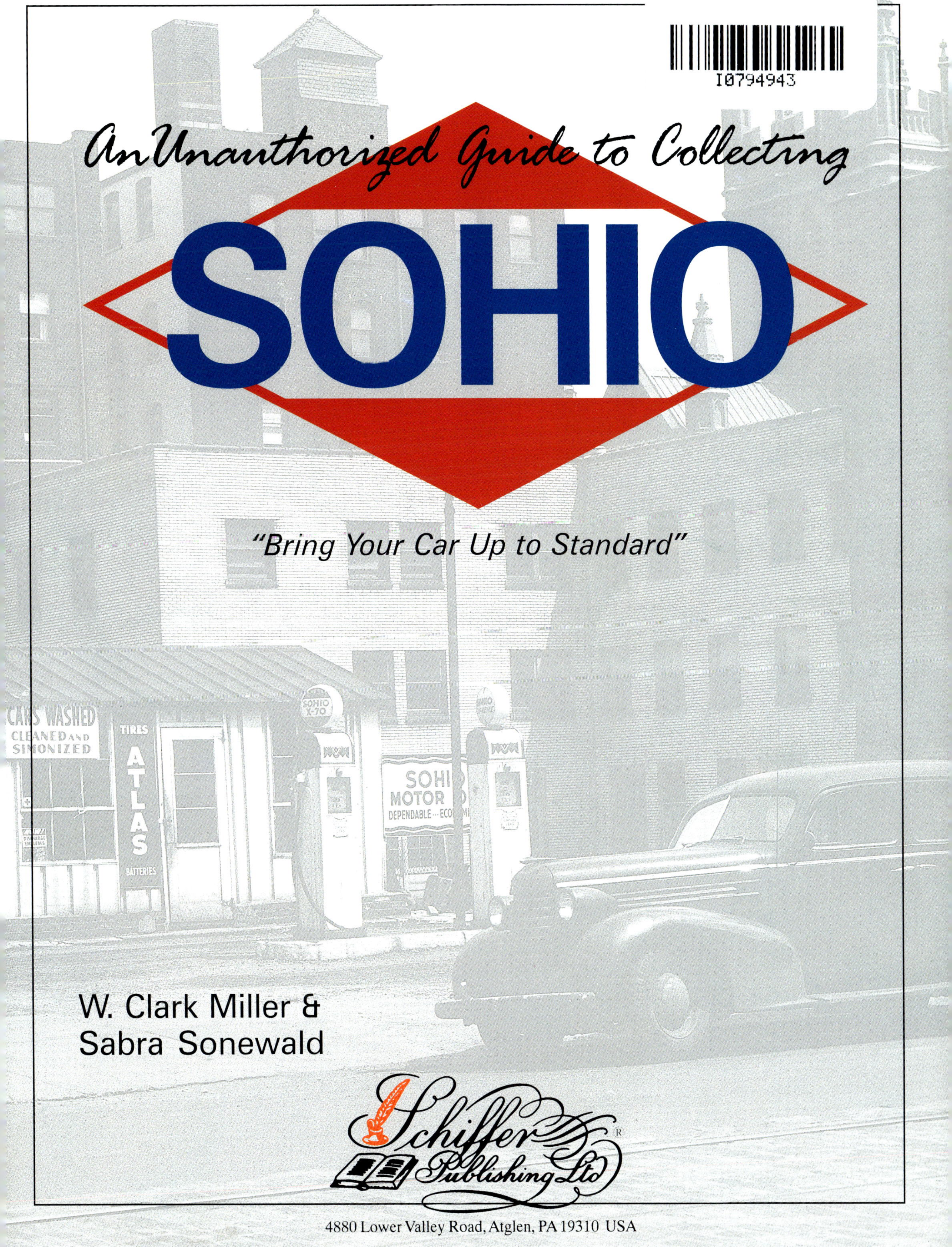

An Unauthorized Guide to Collecting SOHIO

"Bring Your Car Up to Standard"

W. Clark Miller &
Sabra Sonewald

Schiffer Publishing Ltd
4880 Lower Valley Road, Atglen, PA 19310 USA

Dedication

This book is dedicated to my Dad, Clark O. Miller, who never discouraged me from collecting in the early years and even helped add to my collection. My father was a chemical engineer who formulated additives for oil products for many oil companies such as Pure, Atlantic, Gulf and Standard Oil of Ohio (SOHIO). His hard work and constant dedication made great improvements in many of the oil products that we use today. His lifelong passion for improving product performance forced all oil companies to develop better brands, stricter standards and the highest quality. Second, to my friend and partner, Sabra Sonewald, whose help has enriched and expanded my collection. Last, to my fellow collectors, who make this hobby enjoyable for everyone, spending their time, talent, and resources to keep alive a vital part of American automotive history.

W. Clark Miller

My contributions to this book are dedicated to my father, E. John Sonewald, who recently passed away with cancer. He was extremely excited about this book but never lived to see its completed form. He was a loving and supportive father and a good friend. I continue to marvel at his inquisitive nature concerning all things scientific and am proud to dedicate the book to his memory.

Sabra Sonewald

This book was compiled without the knowledge or permission from British Petroleum Co., of which Sohio and all product names are registered trademarks, and also without the knowledge of or permission from Atlas Supply Company, of which "Atlas" is a registered trademark. This book is compiled entirely from the author's collection and collections of others.

Library of Congress Catalog Card Number: 99-69100

Book Design by Anne Davidsen
Type set in Zurich

ISBN: 0-7643-1103-4

Printed in China
1 2 3 4

Published by Schiffer Publishing Ltd.
4880 Lower Valley Road
Atglen, PA 19310
Phone: (610) 593-1777; Fax: (610) 593-2002
Please visit our web site catalog at
www.schifferbooks.com
or write for a free catalog.
This book may be purchased from the publisher.
Please include $3.95 for shipping.

In Europe, Schiffer books are distributed by
Bushwood Books
6 Marksbury Ave.
Kew Gardens
Surrey TW9 4JF England
Phone: 44 (0)208 392-8585; Fax: 44 (0)208 392-9876
E-mail: Bushwd@aol.com
Free postage in the UK. Europe: Air mail at cost.
Please try your bookstore first.

We are interested in hearing from authors
with book ideas on related subjects.

Table of Contents

Acknowledgements

The author would like to acknowledge the following people for their help, input, and lending of their collections: Mr. Norm Griffin, Mr. Roger Hubbell, Bill & Carla Sigworth, Mr. Scott Benjamin, Mr. Bill Killian, Mr. J. Sam McIntyre, Tom and Char Whitlatch, and last, but not least, the rest of my fellow collectors for their help, leads, and encouragement. Also thanks to Mike Axel at Axel Photography.

Introduction

I have been interested in service stations as long as I can remember. My dad worked for Lubrizol Corporation in Cleveland developing additives for gasoline, motor oils, and other types of fuels and lubricants. From time to time, he would bring home containers of products that had his additives in them. I guess I liked all the different brands and graphics of the cans and the fact that they contained his product. My interest in this field grew from picking up small cans, maps and other paper items on family vacations to begging my mom to stop at local gas stations we never dealt with so I could pick up empty cans to add to my collection. I have amassed a sizeable quantity; I still have about 100 of these cans in my collection. I got away from this pastime and went on to other things over the years. Then, about 15 years ago, I got hooked again after going to a local antique show and picking up a couple of items. That was all it took to get my interest sparked again. What started as an interest has grown into a full-blown passion and a collection of 8,000-plus pieces of service station history. My main interest is containers of all sizes and products, and items of all kinds from Standard Oil of Ohio (SOHIO). Why SOHIO? I have been asked this question many times. I guess SOHIO is the station we always dealt with for gasoline and auto repairs, as did a lot of Ohioans. So it is a nostalgia thing, as with a lot of collecting areas these days. In this book, I will share my knowledge and collection with you as well as the collections and expertise of others. On this tour through history, you will experience containers, maps, signs, thermometers, and much more. I have tried to date each item as accurately as possible. In some cases the exact date can be determined. In other cases the dates are approximated using the period of time that the design or logo was in use. I also have included any important information in each photo's caption. The prices quoted for each item is an estimate only as condition, rarity, and regionality have a direct impact on prices of these and collectibles in general. I will leave that up to you, the collector. In closing, I hope this book is a valuable addition to your library.

A History of Sohio

In 1911, the U.S. Supreme Court ordered Standard of New Jersey to divest itself of holdings in 33 other companies, forming Standard Oil of Ohio as a one-state marketer. Sohio, as it emerged from the breakup, was the much pared-down remnant of Rockefeller's original creation, and it seems the court took particular vengeance on the company. Sohio was left with only the Cleveland refinery and marketing throughout Ohio. Making the most of what it had, Sohio concentrated on becoming a market leader. Sohio was among the first to consider retail gasoline marketing a viable business function for a refiner-marketer. The company's bulk plants and sales offices throughout Ohio gave it the basis for the most retail-minded business philosophy of any of the Standard companies.

Sohio was assigned the Standard, Red Crown, and Polarine brand names for use in Ohio only. It was operating a drive-though fueling facility at a Columbus bulk plant within a year of the breakup and by 1916 had pioneered a standardized station design, known as Type A, suitable for all types of locations, from which Red Crown gasoline and Polarine oil could be dispensed. Sohio was content to buy crude from outside sources in the early years and had sufficient marketing to support the construction of a new refinery in Toledo in the early 1920s. Crude oil developments actually harmed Sohio's profitability. Rich in domestic crude and with excess refining capacity, Midwestern marketers such as Sinclair entered Ohio markets to wrest away some of Sohio's 80 percent-plus shares of the state's gasoline market, knowing full well that being "brand-locked" as a one state marketer, Sohio had no means of retaliation in its core markets and no auxiliary markets to fall back on. As other marketers discovered Sohio's dilemma, the Ohio market, with its industrial base and relatively high numbers of motorists, attracted many new entrants to gasoline marketing.

To counteract the effects of increasing competition, Sohio elected to turn its sales force into a highly-trained and highly-motivated retail marketing organization, making filling stations operate much like chain stores such as A&P. A new image was developed, as red-white-and-blue had been adopted by many other Standard affiliates and had come to represent Standard gasoline nationwide, as did the marketing brand name Sohio, taken from the corporate name "The Standard Oil Company (Sohio)". Station personnel received a vigorous indoctrination with company marketing philosophy, and Sohio stations became very profitable retail stores for purchasing automotive fuels and oils. Sohio was among the first to add service bays to most of its stations and actively participated in the cooperative formed in 1930 by various Standard affiliates and Atlas Corporation to market automotive items, known in the trade as TBA (Tires, Batteries, and Accessories). Backed by a nationwide guarantee with warranty service available through virtually all of the stations that had repair facilities that bore the various brands of Standard of Ohio, New Jersey, California, Indiana, and Kentucky, Atlas gave these companies a TBA line they could call their own and made the term "filling station" obsolete, allowing filling stations to truly become "service stations".

Sohio, too, was among the first marketers to develop a "super-station" concept. Thwarted only be excessive cost and low returns during the Depression, the fabulous Sohio "English Lodge" stations expanded on Pure's successful cottage design then in use by adding service areas and customer lounges like those found in upscale department stores. A number of these units were built, but cost restrictions of the Depression era prevented this new marketing concept to fully take shape.

Although Sohio could not use its valued Standard-related trademarks outside Ohio, nothing prevented the company from entering other markets under other brand names. Sohio chose the route of purchasing existing marketing operations, the first of which was Wheeling, West Virginia-based Spears and Riddle. Spears and Riddle was a wholesale marketer, essentially a terminal company, that distributed gasoline from New York to the Gulf Coast. Independent marketers purchasing from Spears and Riddle were offered use of the brand name Fleet-Wing. When Sohio completed the purchase, its established the Fleet-Wing Corporation, based in Cleveland, Ohio, as a brand of independent jobbers in Pennsylvania, West Virginia, Michigan and Ohio in limited numbers. This split operation—corporate Sohio stations and jobber Fleet-Wing stations—served to foster the image of two separate companies to those motorists who preferred not to do business with a Standard company. Moreover, it made Sohio less dependent on Ohio markets and gave it a brand to retaliate with out-of-state marketeers.

Next came Refiners Oil Company, the Dayton, Ohio-based markets in southern Ohio and southeastern Indiana. Refiners had been the original distributor of Ethyl gasoline, when Dayton-based General Motors Research Labs needed a company through which to test market its tetraethyl lead additive. Although Indiana Standard and Jersey Standard would come to dominate the Ethyl operation, Jersey being a partner in the creation of Ethyl Gasoline Corporation, it was tiny Refiners Oil that had led the way. Refiners' more than 250 stations were re-branded Sohio in 1930.

During the 1930s, Sohio sought out ways to offset the effects of the Depression by shifting profit centers to those areas not so dependent upon the ordinary consumer. Sohio purchased a Standard sibling, Solar Refining, increasing its refining capacity and solidifying its refining position. Sohio began developing a pipeline network both for crude oil gathering and product distribution, minimizing the company's transportation costs and allowing it to make spot market purchases of crude where pricing advantages arose.

Recovery was successful, and nearly complete, when World War II erupted. Sohio, as a manufacturer of sorts, joined the wartime effort to manufacture badly needed aviation fuels and lubricants and was a leading supplier of these fuels to the armed services. Crude exploration and production was intensified as well, in support of the refineries and their efforts. When the war ended, Sohio returned to its position as Ohio's dominant gasoline marketer, and post war expansion and service station development was intensified. Sohio stations of the area sported a distinctive art moderne look and differed from competing stations with an open-air design that did not partition off automotive service areas from sales offices and showrooms.

In another marketing expansion move, Sohio purchased Canfield, Ohio-based Canfield Oil Company. Founded in 1886, Canfield originally had been a lubricants manufacturer. Its Wm. Penn motor oils were among the first branded oils to be distributed over a large region of the country and were highly regarded as one of the top-quality motor oils in the early automotive era. At the time of the Sohio purchase, Canfield branded more than 200 stations in Ohio and Pennsylvania. Sohio operated Canfield stations, later Wm. Penn stations, as a secondary brand until the 1980s. In the early 1960s, an effort was made to establish the Wm. Penn brand of motor oils as an automotive jobber brand; that is, one that was sold primarily through auto parts distributors. The plan was never widely accepted, although Wm. Penn oils were marketed until after the BP brand replaced Sohio brands in 1990.

In the early 1950s, Sohio was among the first of the major oil companies to look beyond lubricants into other petrochemical products, particularly those for agricultural use. Existing sales channels were available, and Sohio chemical products became well known throughout the state. Sohio was also the first marketer to discover that by adding the chemical element boron to gasoline, antiknock performance was improved and engine wear was reduced. In 1954, Sohio introduced Sohio Boron Supreme, replacing Sohio Supreme as its premium grade product. Two years later, Sohio decided to enter markets outside Ohio with company-owned, retail-oriented station in areas where its affiliate brands, Fleet-Wing and Canfield, had been successful. To avoid directly identifying its jobber brands with Sohio, company stations outside Ohio displayed the brand name boron on station signage. Boron Oil became a Sohio subsidiary and the first Boron signs were installed at stations in the Kentucky suburbs of Cincinnati, where Sohio operated a refinery. The brand was expanded several years later, as Boron stations appeared in West Virginia and Pennsylvania, particularly the Pittsburgh area. These would become strongholds for the Boron brand in years to follow.

When the brand name Sohio was introduced in 1928, station signage consisted of an oval with a diamond-like design forming triangles over the word "Sohio" on a center band. The logo saw several revisions but by 1960 was looking somewhat dated. In addition, the signs did not reproduce well for use in the large signage needed at interstate off-ramps. In 1962, Sohio introduced a new logo, an oval shield with an inner oval bearing either the Sohio or Boron brand names. Stations were re-imaged as well, and many received a new design with side entry bays, hiding automotive work from direct roadside view allowing more decorative landscaping then being mandated by many metropolitan zoning boards. The new logo was incorporated into station design as well and was proudly displayed on structural walls.

The Boron brand grew rapidly in the early 1960s and by 1968, Boron entered Michigan markets and was being added to a number of truck stop facilities and other unconventional service stations of the era. Tie-ins with food service and lodging operations, although not unusual in the 1960s, seemed to indicate something of the look of today's convenience store/fast food combination units. Sohio's retail orientation and chain of company-operated stations gave them opportunity to experiment with various marketing concepts, some of which led to today's service station designs. To ensure a consistent image, the company opted to concentrate primarily on company-owned and operated or company-owned, dealer-leased stations. Sohio sold off the Fleet-Wing operation to Pennzoil in 1968. Fleet-Wing stations in Ohio, West Virginia, and Pennsylvania were eventually converted to the Pennzoil brand, virtually all of them prior to 1980.

In spite of its success in the retail marketplace, Sohio suffered from lack of crude oil production. By the 1960s, Sohio was involved in some domestic production, alone or in combination with other companies. Its crude-gathering pipeline network led from all major production fields to its refineries. Still Sohio was little more than a regional oil company, standing below such regional entities as Pure, Union, and DX in assets, sales and profits. Sohio management saw the wisdom in growth and self-sufficiency and in the growth-through-merger days of the 1960s, Sohio began to look for a crude-rich partner with which to team up.

British Petroleum was founded as an exploration company in the early years of this century and was owned in part by the British government. Very successful and profitable, British Petroleum, commonly called BP, was a world leader in petroleum by the time it entered North American markets in the late 1950s with a small number of stations in Canada. In the late 1960s, BP exploration tenacity paid off, and with two huge oil discoveries in Alaska, BP was inundated with crude oil. BP entered United States markets after purchasing from Atlantic Richfield the former Sinclair marketing along the eastern seaboard from Maine to Florida, along with some surplus Atlantic locations in the Northeast. BP signs were first erected at stations in this county in Atlanta, Georgia, in 1969.

Sohio had found its partner. In 1970, Sohio traded a minority interest with increases in ownership tied to crude oil production—British Petroleum in exchange for BP's U.S. marketing subsidiary NP Oil. The deal was mutually beneficial in that BP gained refinery capacity, access to pipelines and a foothold in the huge U.S. gasoline market. Of the Sinclair locations it had purchased, many were old and poorly located. Sinclair had done little in the way of developing an interstate marketing operation, preferring to brand small jobber-supplied stations on Main Street in every town east of the Rockies. By 1973, BP was in the process of selling off many of the stations and supply agreements in the Southeast, primarily to American Petrofina. Fina signs replaced BP signs at hundreds of stations. The remaining BP marketing network was within economical supply reach of Sohio refineries and pipelines. In one of the few market expansion moves by the company in the 1970s, Sohio purchased McLean, Virginia-based Scot Stations. Scot operated high-volume discount super pumpers in the Washington-Baltimore metropolitan area, as well as around Richmond and Norfolk. Successful outlets were eventually converted to the BP brand, although Sohio operated the Scot chain until the early 1980s. Also added to the Sohio retail presences was the Truckstops of America operation. TA, as it was commonly known, had seen several owners in the previous years, but with access to oil company reserves, both financially and product related, TA was finally in a position to solidify its place among the nation's truck stop operators.

As BP ownership in Sohio increased and Sohio's crude oil supply problems subsided, market expansion again became a corporate interest. When Chevron merged with Gulf in 1984, the Gulf marketing in the Southeast overlapped the existing Chevron marketing in the former Kyso states. To avoid antitrust action, the Gulf marketing in eight southeastern states, the stations and jobber supply contracts were sold to Sohio, with a license to use the Gulf logo for a minimum of five years. The beginning of 1985 found Sohio operating stations under brands Sohio, Boron, BP, Scot, Wm. Penn, TA, Gulf, Gas and Go (a trademark introduced as a secondary brand at former Boron outlets in Michigan), and Gibbs (a New England jobber brand that BP had inherited as a secondary brand in the Sinclair purchase).

117 years after John D. Rockefeller consolidated his petroleum operations into Cleveland, Ohio-based Standard Oil, his original operation known as Standard Oil Company of Ohio ceased to exist as a corporate entity. The year was 1987, and British Petroleum, exercising an option dating back to the original merger with Sohio, purchased the remaining portions of the company. Standard Oil Company of Ohio became BP America. Much speculation was made about the eventual choice of brand names to be used, particularly among Gulf jobbers and dealers in the Southeast. Gulf was the most well-respected brand in some parts of the south and any change needed to be thought out carefully. Prior to

1987, Sohio had originally intended to eventually replace Gulf with Boron and had already expanded that brand into new territory with some Boron stations in Virginia. With the BP purchase in 1987, the plans changed as it became apparent that the BP brand, familiar only through its use on former Sinclair outlets, would replace not only Gulf, but Boron and the other brands as well. "Would the Sohio brand be spared?" was a question headlining several trade publications. Sohio, identified for more than sixty years with its home state Ohio, had been, perhaps, the perfect gasoline trademark. Sohio stations were the most familiar commercial site in Ohio. If BP were to replace Sohio, would it have any lasting effects?

Nashville, Tennessee, was chosen as the test market for the new BP brand. Prior to this time, Gulf, Sohio, and Boron stations had received a re-imaging, with station components fashioned from silver panels and the respective logos displayed on a green background. In the summer of 1989, all Gulf outlets in Nashville and Davidson County, Tennessee, were converted to BP brand and the complete BP image package was displayed to the buying public for the first time. Motorists reacted favorably, so beginning with a single station in Marshall, North Carolina, in May 1990, Gulf stations in eight states were converted to BP in five months of re-branding and re-imaging. Atlas products, inherited by BP from Sohio, became available to former Gulf jobbers, who tended to remain strong in TBA items. Boron outlets and the other brands were converted to BP in 1990 as well. The following year, 1991, Ohio lost its namesake landmarks as the BP brand replaced Sohio, again in a summer re-branding and re-imaging.

BP America, as a successor to Standard Oil Company of Ohio, is today a fully integrated unit of British Petroleum and ranks eighth in assets and ninth in number of stations, with nearly 7,000 branded outlets in twenty-seven states including some West Coast stations where the BP brand was franchised to West Coast independent Tosco.

Thanks to Scott Benjamin and Wayne Henderson for contributing this brief history.

BP Changeover

After 61 years of being a standard fixture on every Ohio road from April 1929 to February 1989, the Sohio name was replaced with the yellow and green BP shield. This re-branding included Boron stations in Michigan and Pennsylvania.

This was the final stage of what had been a slow changeover of Sohio, Boron, and Gulf stations in the southeast and BP stations in the northeast, which were rebranded from Sinclair in 1970. This project included 8,000 stations in 26 states, at a cost of at least 100 million dollars.

Also, Standard Oil Production Company and Standard Alaska Production Company were renamed BP Exploration.

The changeover in Ohio was slow but sure. First, full service stations at some prime locations were torn down and rebuilt with the convenience stores of today, done up in blue and silver. Later, the blue trim was replaced with green. Smaller stations were rebranded or closed altogether and sold to other oil companies. In other cases, the dealer was bought out and the property was sold for other uses.

In the final outcome, the reimaged Sohio logo was the only trace of Sohio left on the roadside. This would also become history on February 1, 1989.

Motor Oil Cans
1-quart, 5-quart, 1-gallon, 5-gallon

Standard Gas Engine Oil, 5-gallon can, 1910. $50-75

Polarine Motor Oil, 1-gallon can, 1910. $125-250

Polarine Motor Oil, 2-quart can, 1910. $65-150

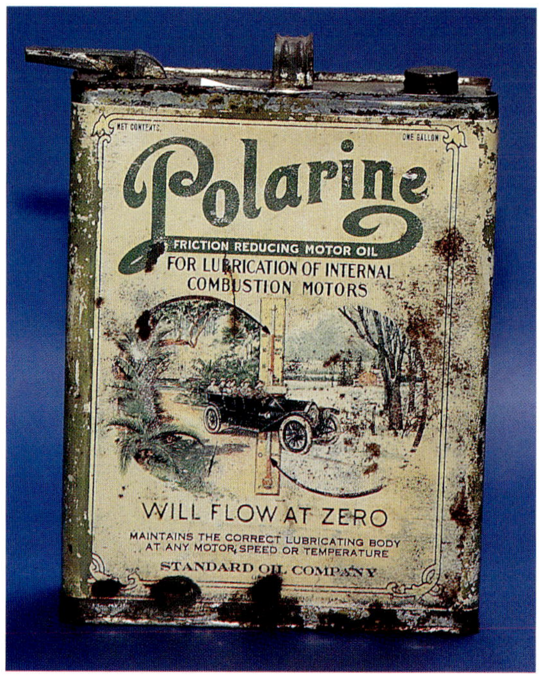

Polarine Motor Oil, 1-gallon can, 1915. $125-250

Polarine Motor Oil, 1-gallon can, 1911-1928. $100-200

Sohio oil bottles, 1 quart, 1930-1950. $250-350 each

Sohio oil bottle, 1 quart, 1930-1950. $225-325

Esso motor oil bottle, 1 quart, 1930-1950. $225-325

Left: Sohio motor oil can case, 1962-1967. $10-25.
Right: Esso motor oil can case, 1952-1962. $10-25 each

Sohio HQD 5-quart can cases, 1951-1962. $10-25 each

Sohio 1-quart oil can cases, holds 24, 1955-1962. $10-25 each

Standard Oil Penn, 5-quart can, 1934-1938. $75-125

Acme Motor Oil, 5-gallon can, 1934. $40-70

Standard Oil Penn, 1-quart can, 1938-1945. $75-125

Standard Oil Penn, 5-quart can, 1938-1945. $75-125

Sohio HQ, 1-quart cans, March 1947-September 1947. $75-125

Far Left: Sohio HQ, 1-gallon can, September 1947-1951. $25-50

Left: Sohio Motor Oil, 5-gallon can, 1931. $40-60

Sohio Motor Oil. Left: 1-quart can, 1940-July 1946, $45-75.
Right: 5-quart can, 1938-July 1946, $50-125.00.

Sohio Motor Oil, 1-quart cans, with patent numbers, 1938-1940. $35-65

Left: Sohio Motor Oil with Pentosul, July 1946-1950, $25-35.
Right: Sohio Motor Oil, 1955-1960, $25-35.

Sohio Motor Oil, tall quart cans, 1930-1938. $150-225 each

Sohio Motor Oil with Pentosul, 1-gallon can, July 1946-1950. $25-45

Left: Sohio HQD, 1-quart can, July 1951-1955, $20-35.
Right: Sohio HQD, 1-quart can, 1955-1962, $20-35.

Left: Sohio Motor Oil, 1-quart can, 1962-1964, $20-30.
Right: Sohio Motor Oil, Boron Oil Co., Cleveland, OH, 1964-1967, $20-30.

Sohio Motor Oil, Non Detergent, 1-quart can, 1960-1962. $30-40

Sohio HQD, 1-gallon can, July 1951-1955. $30-50

Sohio HQD, 5-quart can, 1955-1962. $25-45

Left: Sohio HQD, 1-quart can, 1962-1964, $35-45.
Right: Sohio HQD, aluminum 1-quart can, 1960, $30-40.

Left: Sohio HQD, 1-quart can heavy duty motor oil, 1964-1965, $20-30 Right: Sohio HQD, 1965-1967, $30-40.

Sohio HQD, 1-gallon can, 1962-1964. $20-30

Sohio Sixty Two, 1-quart can, 1967-1972. Replaced HQD in 1967 for cars 1962 and older. $35-75

Sohio HQD, plastic bottle, 1979. HQD name reintroduced for a short period of time as a 30W oil—for use in diesel-powered cars. $10-25

Sohio Premex, 1 quart can, February 25, 1955-1962.
$25-40

Sohio Premex, 5-quart can, July 1955-1962. $20-40

Top: Sohio Premex, silver stripes, 1965-1967, $25-35.
Bottom left: Sohio Premex, newer logo, 1962-1964, $25-35.
Bottom right: Sohio Premex, gold stripes,1964-1965, $30-50.

Sohio Premex, 1-gallon can, 1962-1964. $25-35

Sohio Premcx, 1-quart can, 3 variations, 1967-1970. $25-35

Sohio Premex, 1-quart cans.
Top: 1971-1978, Bottom left: 1978-1983,
Bottom right: 1983-1989. $20-30 each

Sohio Duron, 1-gallon can, 1962-1964. $25-35

Left: Premex, 1-gallon can, 1965-1967, $30-40.
Right: Sohio Premex, 1-gallon can, 1969, $30-40

Left: Sohio Duron, 1-quart can, 1962-1964, $25-35.
Right: Sohio Duron, 1-quart can, 1964-1965, $30-50.

Sohio Duron, 1-gallon can, 1964-1965, $30-50.

Sohio QVO, 1-quart cans. Bottom left: 1968-1969—World's Finest. Bottom right: 1969-1972. Top: 1972-1975. $25-35 each

Sohio QVO, 1-gallon can, 1972-1975. $25-35

Sohio Golden Duron, 1-quart cans. Top: 1965-1969. Bottom left: 1969-1973. Bottom right: 1973-1976. $25-35 each

Left: Sohio QVO 1-quart can, 1975-1983, $15-25.
Right: Sohio QVO, 1 quart can, 1983-1989, $15-25

Sohio Nitrex, 1-quart cans. 1976-1981 (left), 1981-1989 (right). $20-35 each

Sohio Nitrex, 1-gallon can, 1979. $30-40

Left: Sohio Nitrex, Late 1979, $15-25. Right: Nitrex Turbo D, 1980, $15-25.

Above:
2-quart Sohio Bulk Oil Dispenser, 1930s. $250-350

Left:
Left: Nitrex MPG, 1-quart can, 1980, $15-25. Right: Nitrex MPG, 1-quart plastic bottle, 1980, $10-20.

Esso

In 1934 Sohio started marketing Esso Motor Oil through an agreement with Standard Oil Co. of NJ (Esso). This practice continued until 1962.

Left: Esso Motor Oil, 1-quart can, 1934-1939, $35-50.
Right: Esso Motor Oil, 5-quart can, 1934-1939, $45-65.

Esso Motor Oil, 1-quart bottle, 1942-1945. $50-75

Esso Motor Oil, 1-quart can, 1939-1947. $35-45

Esso Motor Oil, 5-quart can, 1939-1947. $35-45

Left: Esso Motor Oil, 1-quart can, 1947-1949, $25-35.
Right: Esso Extra Motor Oil, 1-quart can, 1949-1950, $25-40.

Esso Extra, 1-quart can, 1950-1961. Note difference in logo and grades. $25-35.

Left: Esso Extra, 1-gallon can, 1953, $25-35.
Right: Esso Extra, 5-quart can, 1956, $25-35.

Esso Uniflo, 1-quart can, 1954-1961. $35-45

2-Gallon Motor Oil Cans

Left: Sohio Renown, 2-gallon can, 1933-October 1935, $75-150. Right: Sohio Renown, 2- gallon can, October 1935-July 1938, $45-85.

Right: Sohio Renown, 2-gallon can, July 1938-November 1941, $35-65.
Left: Sohio Polarine, 2-gallon can, November 1941-1953, $25-45.

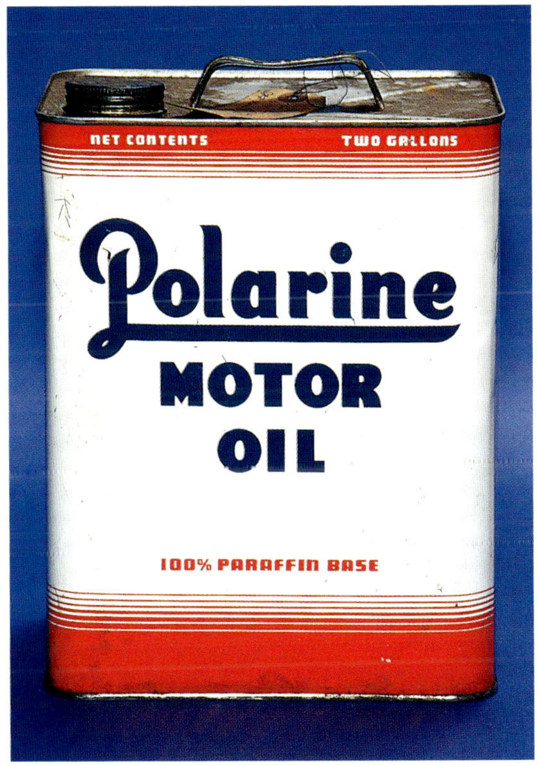

Sohio Polarine, 2-gallon can, 1959-1967, $25-35. This design was packaged in sealed 1 quart cans from 1962-1965. The 1-quart version is very rare, $100-175.

Sohio Polarine, two variations of the 2-gallon can, 1953-1959. $25-45

Outboard Motor Oil

Outboard, 1-quart cans. Left: August 1950-1953, $25-35. Right: 1953-1955, $25-35.

Sohio 7C's, 1-quart can, resealable, 1955-1962. Note variation in logo. $45-75

Sohio 7C's, 1-quart can, 1962-1964. $20-30

Left: Sohio 7C's, 1-quart can, round, 1955-1962, $45-75.
Right: Sohio 7C's, pint can, 1955-1962, $20-40.

Left: Sohio 7C's, 1-quart bottle, 1964-1966, $15-30.
Right: Sohio 7C's, pint bottle, 1964-1969, $15-25.

Sohio 7C's, 1-quart bottle, 1969-1972. $20-30

Sohio 4 Cycle Motor Oil, for use in lawnmowers and other types of power equipment. 1-Quart bottle, 1965-1967, $20-30.

7C's Outboard, 7C's Incorporated, Cleveland, OH, 1960. $25-35

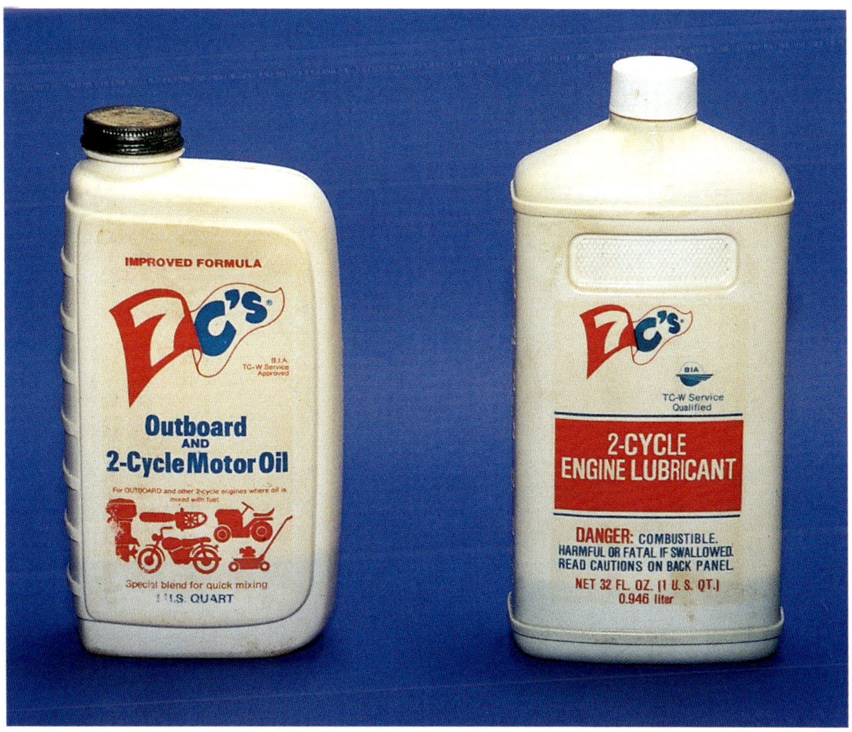

Left: 7C's Outboard, 1-quart plastic bottle, 1972-1977, $10-20.
Right: 7C's Outboard, plastic bottle, 1977-1980, $10-20.

Automatic Transmission Fluid

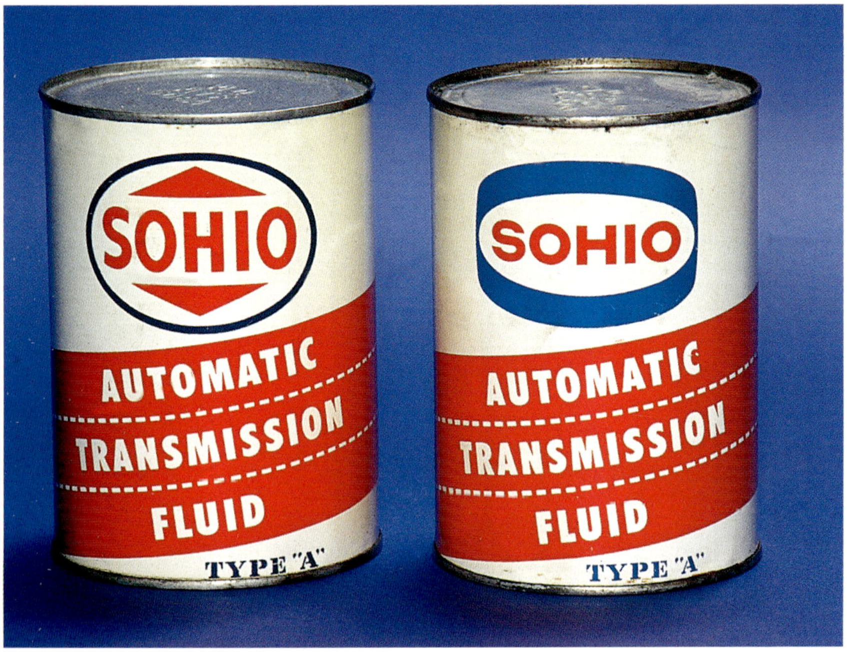

Sohio ATF Type "A", 1-quart cans. Left: 1953-1962, $25-35. Right: 1962-1964, $35-45.

Sohio ATF, 5-quart can, 1953-1962, $25-50.

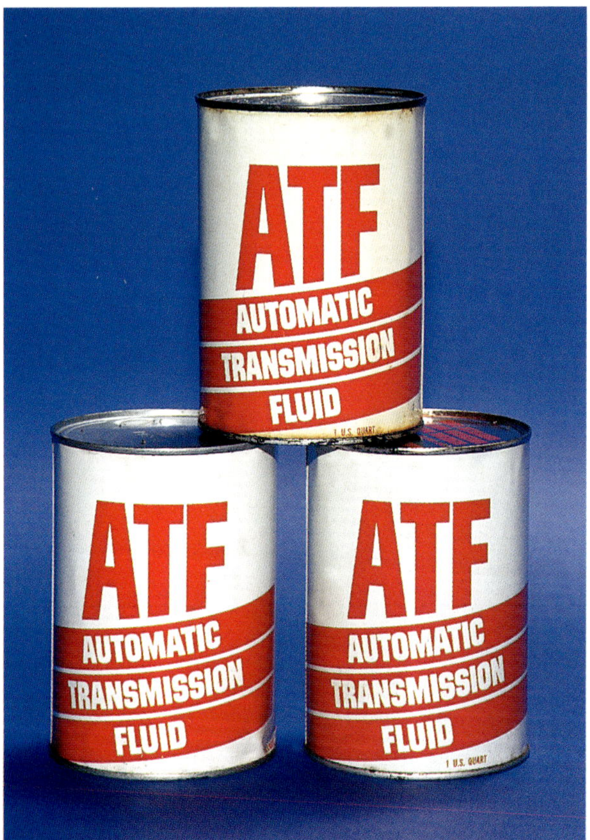

Sohio ATF, 1-quart cans. Top: 1964-1966. Bottom left: 1966-1969. Bottom right: 1969-1973. $25-35 each

Sohio ATF, 1-quart cans, 1974-1990, four variations. $10-20 each

Anti-Freeze

Super Sohio Anti-Freeze, 5-gallon can, 1931. $50-75

Super Sohio Anti-Freeze. Left: 1-quart can, 1935-1940, $50-75. Right: 1-gallon can, 1940-1952, $35-65.

Super Sohio. 1-quart can, 1940-1952. Note chart and logo. $50-75

Super Sohio. 1-quart cans. Top: 1959-1963. Bottom left: 1952-1956. Bottom right: 1956-1959. $25-45 each.

Super Sohio, 1-gallon can, 1952-1956. $25-35

Greases

Sohio Wheel Bearing Grease, 1 lb. tall can , 1928-1934, $45-75.

Sohio Chassis Lubricant, 1-lb. tall can, 1928-1934. $45-75

Sohio Water Pump Grease, 1-lb. tall can, 1928-1934. $45-75

Left: Polarine Cup Grease, 1-lb. can, 1911-1928, $45-65. Right: MICA Axle Grease, 3-lb. can with press-on lid, 1928-1938, $25-40.

MICA Axle Grease, 1-lb. can, 1928-1946. $25-35

Sohio Water Pump Grease, 1-lb. can, 1946. $25-35

Top: Sohio Grease, 1-lb. can, 1944, $25-35. Bottom: Sohio Cup Grease and Sohio Chassis Lubricant, 1-lb. cans, 1955, $25-35.

Sohio Grease, 1-lb. cans, 1935-1946. $25-35 each

Sohio Grease, 1-lb. cans, 1955. $25-35 each

Top: Sohio Tran. #2, 1-lb. can, 1966, $25-35. Right: Sohio Lubtec and Sohio Lubtec L, 1-lb. 1962-February 1964, $25-35 each.

Top: Sohio Lubtec, 1-lb can, October 1956-1962, $20-30.
Bottom: Sohio 1-lb. Grease Cans, 1959-1962, $20-30 (both).

Sohio Grease, 1 lb. cans, 1962. $25-35 each

Polarine Cup Grease, 5-lb. can, 1911-1928. $50-75

Polarine Cup Grease, 5-lb. can, 1928. $25-50

MICA Axle Grease, 5-lb. can, 1928-1945. $25-40

Sohio Mica Axle Grease, 3-lb. can with press-on lid, 1934. $25-35

Sohio Pressure Gun Grease, 5-lb. can, 1935-1945. $25-35

Left: Sohio Cup Grease, 5-lb. can, 1935-1946, $25-35.
Right: Sohio 72 Grease, 5-lb. can, 1930s-1940s, $25-35.

Sohio Water Pump Grease, 1-lb. cans, 1960. $25-35

Sohio Cup Grease, 5-lb. can, 1929. $35-45

Polarine Cup Grease, 10-lb. can, 1911-1928. $50-75

Polarine Cup Grease, 10-lb. can, 1928. $50-100

Sohio Water Pump Grease, 5-lb. can, 1935-1945. $25-35

Sohio Pressure Gun Grease, 5- and 10-lb. cans, 1935-1945. $20-30

Sohio Grease, 10-lb. cans, 1935-1945. $20-30 each

Left: Sohio E-10 Grease, 10-lb. can, 1956, $25-35.
Right: Sohio 911 Grease, 5-lb. can, 1956, $30-40.

Left: Sohio Grease, 10-lb. can, 1960, $25-35.
Right: Sohio Water Pump Grease, 10-lb. can, 1956, $20-30.

Sohio Pressure Gun Grease, 50-lb. keg, 1935-1945. $40-60

Sohio 77 Grease, 10-lb. can. 1959 and 1962. $20-30 each

Left: Sohio Tran. Grease Cartridge, October 1960-1962. $20-30. Right: Sohio Tran. Grease Cartridge, 1962-1964. $20-30

Left: Sohio Lubtec Grease, 10-lb. can, 1959, $20-30.
Right: Sohio Lubtec L Grease, 10-lb. can, 1962, $20-30.

Sohitac Spray Grease, 16 oz., 1960. $15-25

Sohitac Spray Grease,
16-oz. can, 1962. $15-20

Transmission, Gear & Specialty Oils

Polarine Transmission Oil, 1-gallon can, 1927. $100-200

Polarine Spring Oil,
pint can, 1928. $75-125

Polarine Transmission Oil B, 10-lb. can, 1911-1928. $50-100

Polarine Transmission Oil, 5-gallon can, 1928. $40-60

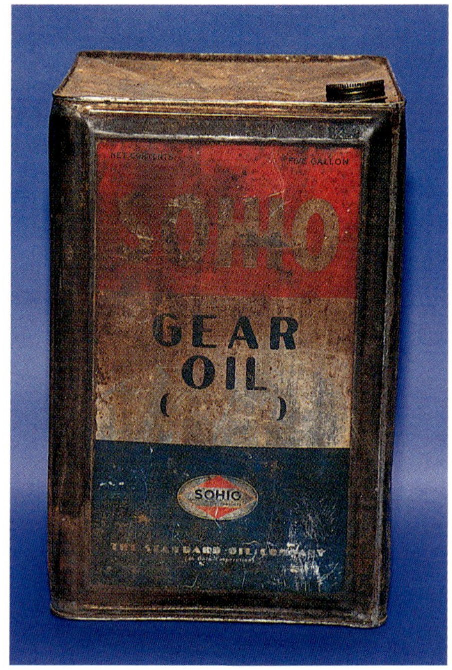

Sohio Gear Oil, 5-gallon can, 1931. $30-50

Sohio Gear Oil, 1-gallon cans, 1928-1946. $35-65 each

Left: Sohio 5-gallon Bulk Can (Sohiolube), 1945, $25-35.
Right: Sohio 25-lb. pail Sohiolube Summer, 1935-1945, $25-45.

Top: Sohiolube Gear Oil, 25 lbs., 1946, $30-50.
Bottom: Sohiolube Gear Oil, 5-gallon can, 1946 and 1947, $25-35 each

Sohio S-W Gear Oil, SAE 90, 1-gallon can, 1960. $25-45

Sohio Gear Oil, 1-gallon cans, 90 and 140 weight, 1956. $25-45 each

Sohio Gear Oil, 1-gallon can, 1961. $25-35

Household Items

Oils and Lighter Fluid

Oil It Home Oiler, 4-oz. can, 1911-1928. $45-75

Sohio Household Oil, 4 oz. cans, 1938 and 1935. $50-75

Sohio Household Oil, 4-oz. can, 1938. $75-150

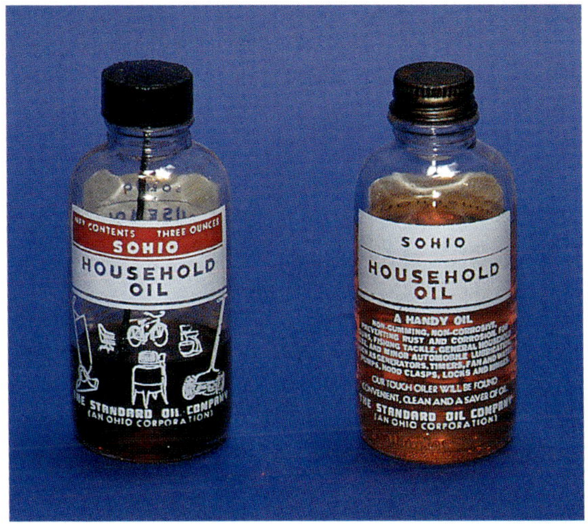

Sohio Household Oil, glass bottle, 1942-1945. $25-45

Left: Sohio Household Oil, 4-oz. can, 1939, $45-75.
Right: Sohio Household Oil, 4-oz. can, $40-70.
Courtesy of Frank's Antiques, Manuta, Ohio.

Sohio Home Oiler, 4-oz. can. Left to right: 1953, 1955, 1959. $25-30 each

Sohio household oil, 4-oz. can, 1956-1958. $25-40

Sohio Home Oiler, 4-oz. can. Left to right: 1959 Experimental Logo, $25-35. 1959-1962, $25-40. 1962-1964, $25-35. 1965, $15-30.

Sohio Soap Box Derby Oil, 4-oz. can. Paper label around 1955 vintage can. $75-125

Sohio Soap Box Derby Oil, 4-oz. can. Paper label around 1962 vintage can. $75-125

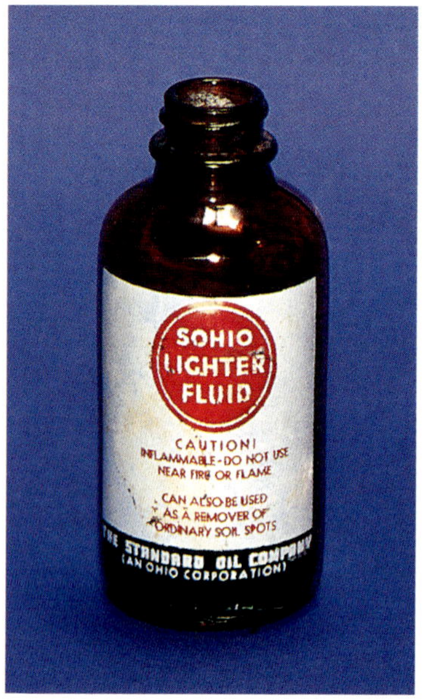

Sohio Lighter Fluid, 4-oz. glass bottle, 1942-1945. $35-45

Sohio Lighter Fluid, 4-oz. can, 1958. No listing. Note the reverse colors in logo. Was this experimental or a printer' s error?

Sohio Lighter Fluid, 4 oz. can. Left: 1949, $35-45. Right: 1950s, two variations, $25-45.

Sohio Lighter Fluid. Left to right: 4-oz. can, 1959-1962, $25-45. 4-oz. can, 1962-1964, $25-45. 4-oz. can, 1965, $25-35. 6-oz. can, 1967, $25-35.

Sohio Penetrating Oil. Left to right: 4-oz. can, 1959, $25-35. 4-oz. can, 1955, $25-35. 4-oz. can with experimental logo, 1958, $25-35.

Sohio Lock Lubricant, 8-oz. can, 1941. $25-50

Left to right: Boron Home Oiler, 4-oz. can, 1968, $15-30. Boron Lighter Fluid, 8-oz. can, 1968, $15-30. Boron Penetrating Oil, 4-oz. can, 1968, $15-30.

Charcoal Starter

Sohio Charcoal Starter, 1/2-gallon can, 1959. $25-30

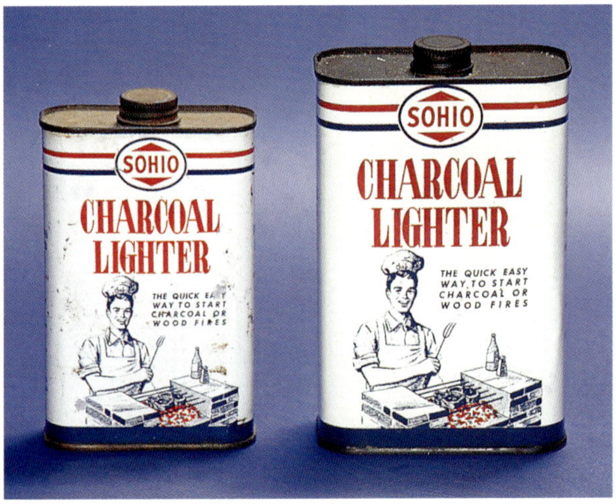

Left: Sohio Charcoal Lighter, 1-quart can, 1956, $20-30.
Right: Sohio Charcoal Lighter, 1-pint can, 1956, $20-30.

Sohio Charcoal Lighter. Left to right: 1-quart can, 1962, $10-20. 1-gallon can, 1965, $10-20. 1-quart can, 1965, $10-20.

Boron Charcoal Lighter. Left: 1-quart can, 1967, $10-20.
Right: 1-gallon can, 1967, $10-20.

Boron Charcoal Lighter. Left: 1-quart can, 1964, $10-20.
Right: 1-quart can, 1965, $10-20.

Boron Charcoal Lighter. Left: 1-quart can, 1979, $5-15.
Right: 1-quart can, 1982, $5-10.

Boron Charcoal Lighter, 1-quart can, 1973. $5-15

Other Products for the Home and Garden

Sohio Dry Cleaner, 2-gallon can. Left: 1956, $20-35. Right: 1959, $20-35.

Sohio Dry Cleaner, 2-gallon can, 1953. $20-35

Sohio Dry Cleaner, 2-gallon can. Left: 1960, $20-30. Right: 1962, $20-30.

Sohio GardenLite, 1-gallon can, 1956. $25-35

Boron Garden Lite, 1-gallon can. Left: 1965, $20-30.
Right: 1962, $20-30.

Sohio Insect Killer, 12-oz. can. Left: 1960, $20-30.
Right: 1962, $20-30.

Left to right: Sohio Insect Spray, 12-oz. can, 1950, $20-30. Sohio Insect Spray, 12-oz. can, 1956, $20-30. Sohio Insect Killer, 12-oz. can, 1958, $20-30.

Left: Sohio Moth Spray, 12-oz. can, 1956, $20-30.
Right: Sohio Moth Proofer, 12-oz. can, 1958, $20-30.

Left to right: Boron Insect Killer, 13-oz. can, 1965, $15-30. Boron Ant & Roach, 13-oz. can, 1969, $15-25. Boron Insect Repellent, 6-oz. can, 1971, $15-25.

Left: Sohio Insect Killer, 13-oz. can, 1964, $15-25. Right: Sohio Ant & Roach, 13-oz. can, 1964, $15-25.

Left: Sohio Aerosol Bomb, 12-oz. can, 1948, $20-30. Right: Sohio Insect Repellent, 8-oz. can, 1946, $20-30.

Sohio Air Spray, 8-oz. can. Left: 1956, $15-30. Right: 1958, $15-30.

Sohio Floor Wax, 1-quart bottle, 1945. $35-55

Sohio Plastic Floor Gloss, 1-quart can, 1959. $25-35

Left: Sohio Supreme Wax Remover, 1-quart can, 1959, $20-30. Right: Sohio Floor Wax, 1-quart can, 1956, $20-30.

Sohio Floor Wax, 1-gallon can, 1938. $25-35

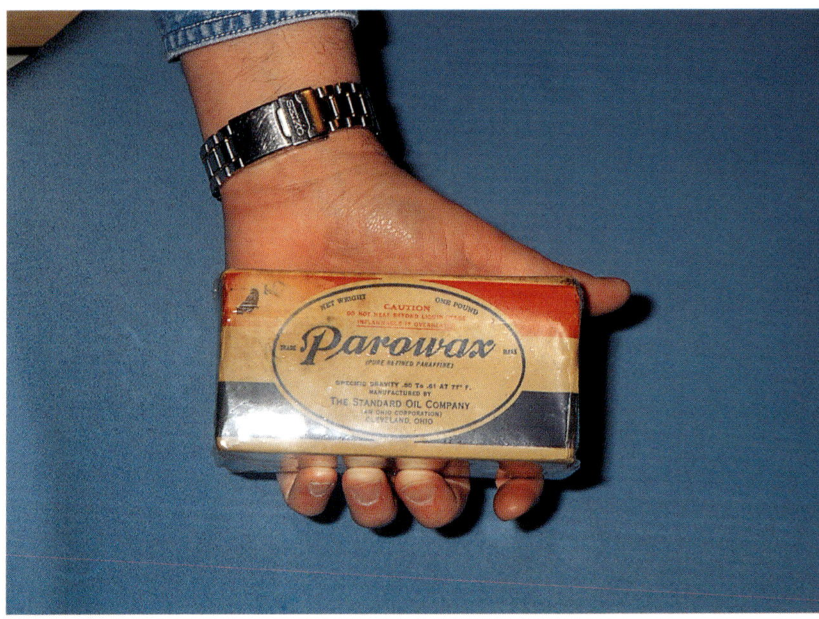

Sohio Parowax, 12-oz. package, 1946. $10-25

Sohio Parowax and Sohio Wax. 12-oz. packages, 1948-1960, $10-20 each.

Sohio Parowax Labels for Canning Jars, 1951. $10-15

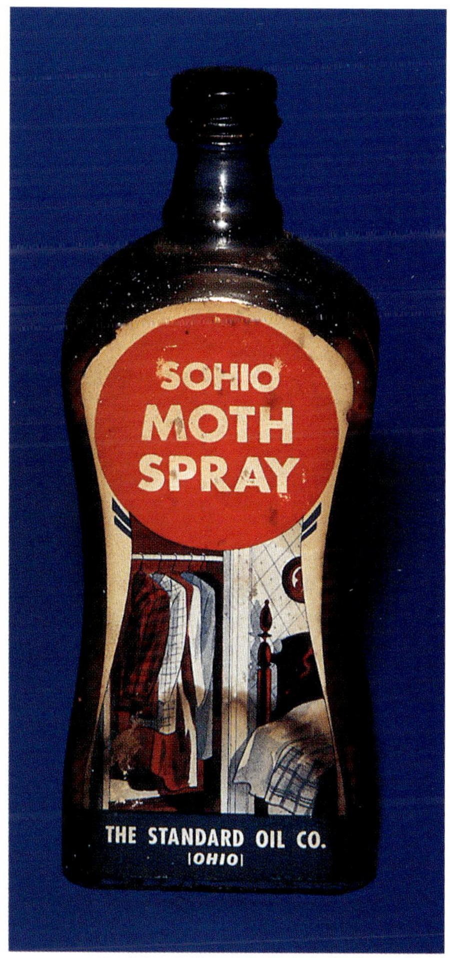

Sohio Moth Spray, pint bottle, 1936, $35-75.

Sohio Parowax, 1-lb. packages, 1968-1970. $5-10 each.
Center: Parowax Candle Kit, 1969, $15-25.

Sohio Disinfectant, 8-oz. bottle, 1936, $25-75.

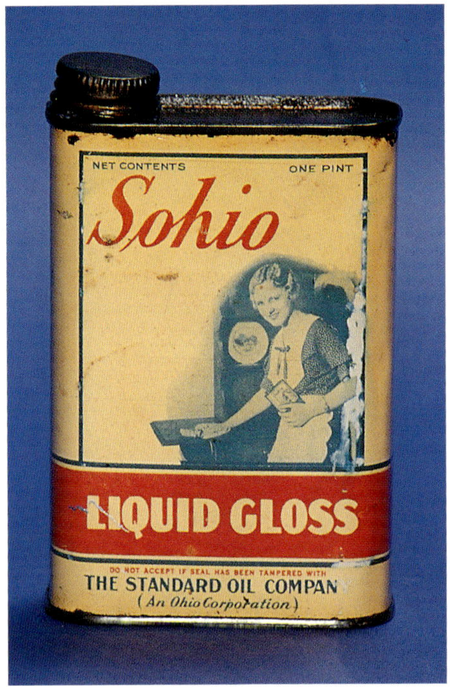

Sohio Liquid Gloss, 1-pint can, 1936. $50-125

Sohio Roach Spray, 1-pint can, 1940. $50-125

Sohio Leather Dressing, pint can, 1940. $40-60

Sohio Glass Cleaner, 1-gallon jug, 1939. $35-60

Sohio Shampoo, 1-pint bottle, 1940. $50-65

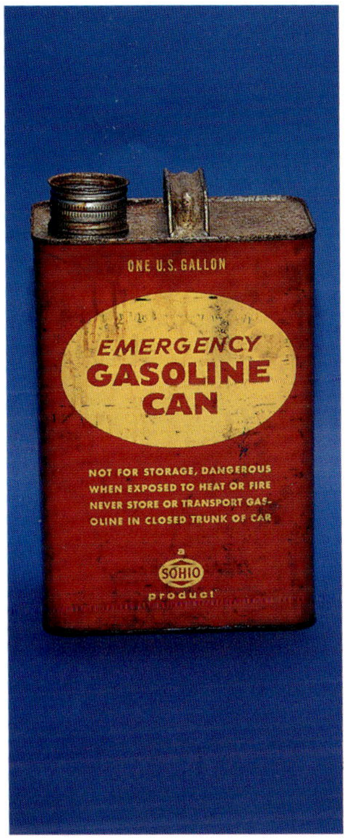

Emergency Gas Can,
1 gallon, 1960. $15-30

Sohio Mineral Oil, 1-quart bottle,
1941. $15-25

Sohio Silicone Spray Lubricant, 8-oz.
can, 1964. $10-15

Gasoline Additives

Sohio HI-CYL Valve Oil, 1-pint can,
1930-1940. $35-65

HI-CYL Valve Oil, 1-pint glass bottle,
May 1947-August 1953. $25-45

Super HI-CYL Valve Oil, 1-pint glass bottle, August 1953-1956, $25-45. Note Logo Variation.

Sohio HI-CYL, 12-oz. cone-top can. Left: White letters, 1957-1959, $20-30. Left: Blue letters, 1956-1957, $20-30.

Sohio Frostex, 12-oz. cone-top can, 1953-1957, $20-30. Right: Sohio Frostex, 12-oz. flat-top can, 1957-1962, $20-30.

Left to right: Sohio Valve Ease, 12-oz. can, 1959-1962, $25-35. Sohio Valve Ease, 12-oz. can, 1962-1966, $25-35. Sohio Valve Ease Concentrate, 8-oz. can, 1966-1973, $15-25.

So-clear Washer Fluid, 1-quart can. Left to right: 1946-1953, $25-35. Right: 1953-1957, two variations, $25-35 each.

Car Care Products

Sohio Windshield Washer Fluid. Left: 6-oz. glass bottle, 1957-1962, $20-35. Center: 1-quart plastic bottle, 1970s, $10-20. Right: 6-oz. glass bottle, 1962-1967, $20-30.

Left to right: Sohio So-clear, glass pint bottle, 1962, $20-30. Sohio Washer Fluid, 1-quart plastic bottle, 1963, $15-25. Sohio Washer Fluid, 1-quart plastic bottle, 1966, $15-25.

Left: Sohio Rapid Car Wash, 1-quart bottle, 1953, $25-35. Right: Sohio Rapid Car Wash, 1-quart bottle, 1955, $25-35.

Rapid Car Wash, 1-quart plastic bottle, 1965. $10-20

Matchless Liquid Gloss, 1/2-pint can, 1911-1928. $25-45

Left: Sohio Liquid Gloss, 1/2-pint can, 1935, $25-45.
Right: Sohio Liquid Gloss, 1-quart can, 1928, $30-50.

Above:
Sohio Liquid Gloss, 1-gallon can, 1928. $45-75

Left:
Reverse of 1928 1-gallon Liquid Gloss can.

Left: Sohio Auto Wax, 8-oz. bottle, 1939, $25-35.
Right: Sohio Auto Polish, 8-oz. bottle, 1941, $25-35.

Left: Sohio Auto Polish, 8-oz. bottle, 1942-1945, $30-40.
Right: Sohio Auto Wax, 8-oz. bottle, 1942-1945, $30-40.

Sohio Auto Polish, plastic pint bottle, 1960. $20-30

Left to right: Sohio Chrome Protector, 8-oz. bottle, 1956, $25-35. Sohio Auto Polish, pint can, 1957, $25-35. Sohio Tar Remover, pint bottle, 1955, $20-30.

Left: Sohio Paste Wax, 1-lb. can. Left: 1960-1962, $25-45. Right: 1962-1964, $25-45.

Sohio Auto Polish, 1-pint can, 1954. $15-30

Sohio Paste Wax, 1-lb. can, 1954, $25-45.

Sohio Waxaid, 4-oz. paper can, 1939. $20-40

Sohio Wax Spray, 12-oz. can, June 1950. Rare, $50-100.

Left: Sohio White Tire Cleaner, 12-oz. bottle, 1956, $25-35.
Right: Sohio Tar Remover, 12-oz. bottle, 1953, $25-45.

Left: Sohio Wash & Shine, 12-oz. spray can, 1961, $15-25.
Right: Sohio Motor Cleaner, 12-oz. spray can, 1962, $15-25.

Sohio Tar Remover, 1-pint can. Left: 1959, $15-30.
Right: 1960, $15-30.

Sohio Tar Remover, 1-pint can. Left: 1962, $15-25.
Right: 1964, $15-25.

Sohio Ice Remover, 12-oz. can. Left: 1960, $15-25. Right: 1962, $15-25.

Left: Sohio Ice Remover, 12-oz. can, 1965, $15-25. Right: Boron Ice Remover, 12-oz. can, 1967, $15-25.

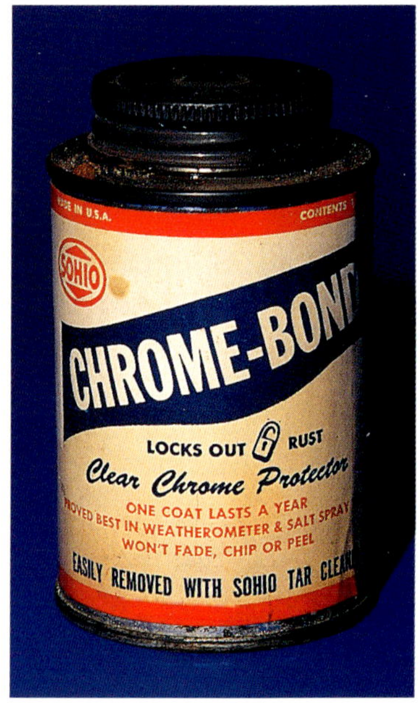

Sohio Chrome Bond Chrome Protector, 8-oz. can, 1955. $15-25

Sohio Handy Sander, 1955, $45-75. These were 1-lb. wax cones filled with sand for emergency winter traction.

Left: Boron Starting Fluid, 11-oz. can, 1963, $10-20.
Right: Boron Starting Fluid, 11-oz. can, 1967, $10-20.

Chapter Three

Products for Special Markets

Farm Products

Left: Sohio HD, 1-qt. can, 1955-1962, $35-65. Right: Sohio HD-S-3, 1-qt. can, 1953-1962, $35-55. Although Sohio HD and HD-S-3 were also commercial products, they were heavily marketed to farmers.

Left: Sohio HD, 1-qt. can, 1962-1964, $35-65. Right: Sohio HD S-3, 1-qt. can, 1962-1964, $35-85.

Sohio Products, 5-gallon can, 1946. This can would be filled with the product of the customer's choice. $50-$75.

Sohio Farmex Quick Fill Grease cans, 1958 and 1954. $35-55 each.

Sohio Ford Tractor Lubricant, 5-gallon cans, 1945 and 1955. For use in Ford 9N and 8N tractors. $50-75 each.

Sohio Farmex Grease, 10-lb. can, 1958. $25-35

Sohio Farmex tractor-mounted grease gun holder with grease tubes. A bonus item for 1959 farm oil deal. $275-375. Farmers were given prizes and free oil and grease for ordering their lubricant needs at the start of the season.

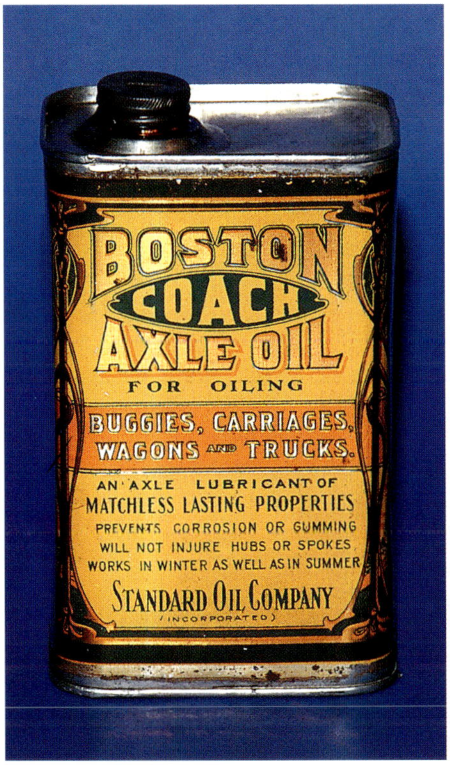

Boston Coach Oil, 1-qt. can, 1920. $75-150

Eureka Harness Oil, 1-gallon can, 1910. $75-150

Left: Eureka Harness Oil, 1-quart can, 1941, $40-60.
Right: Sohio Eureka Harness Oil, 2-quart can, 1938, $40-60.

Left: Eureka Harness Oil, 1-gallon can, 1939, $50-175.
Right: Eureka Harness Oil, 1-gallon can, 1947, $35-75.

Hand Separator Oil. Left to right: 1-quart can, 1941, $40-60. Hand Separator Oil, 2-quart can, 1938, $40-60. 1-gallon can, 1938, $40-75.

Sohio Hand Separator Oil, glass bottle, 1942-1945. $35-75

Sohio Hand Separator Oil, 1-gallon can, 1949. $25-45

Sohio Fly Spray, 1-gallon can, 1946. $25-45

Sohio Herd Oil, 1-gallon can, 1962. $25-45

Sohio Herd Oil, 1-gallon can. Left: 1953, $35-65. Right: 1955, $35-65.

Sohio Hand Separator Oil, 1-gallon can, 1935-1945, $35-65.
Right: Eureka Harness Oil, 1-gallon can, 1935-1945, $35-65.

Left: Sohio Liquid Gloss, 1/2 pint can, 1928-1946, $35-50.
Right: Sohio Penetrating Oil, 1-gallon can, 1928-1946, $35-65.

Sohio Household Oil, 1-gallon can, 1935-1945. $35-65

Sohio Eureka Harness Oil, 2-quart can, 1936-1946. $35-50

Sohio Fly Spray, 1-quart bottle, 1945. $35-55

Left: Sohio Liquid Gloss, 1-gallon can, 1955, $25-35.
Right: Sohio Kleenup, 1-gallon can, 1955, $25-35.

Sohio Weed Killer, 1-gallon can, 1960. $25-35

Sohio Hand Sprayer, 1930s. $25-35

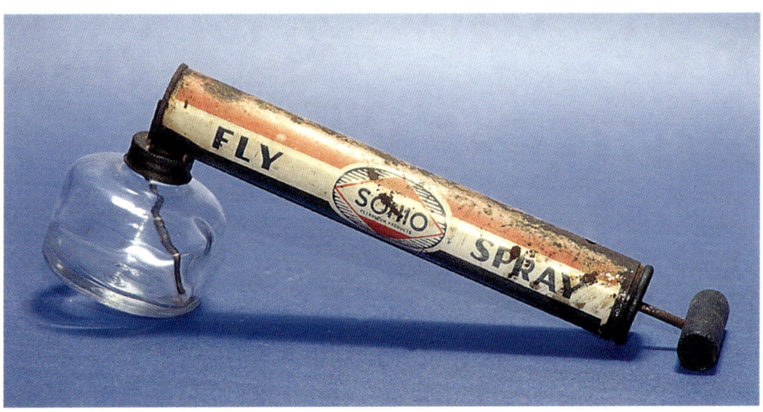

Sohio Sprayer, 9", 1938. $25-35

Sohio Leather Dressing, 1-quart can, 1935-1945.
$35-55

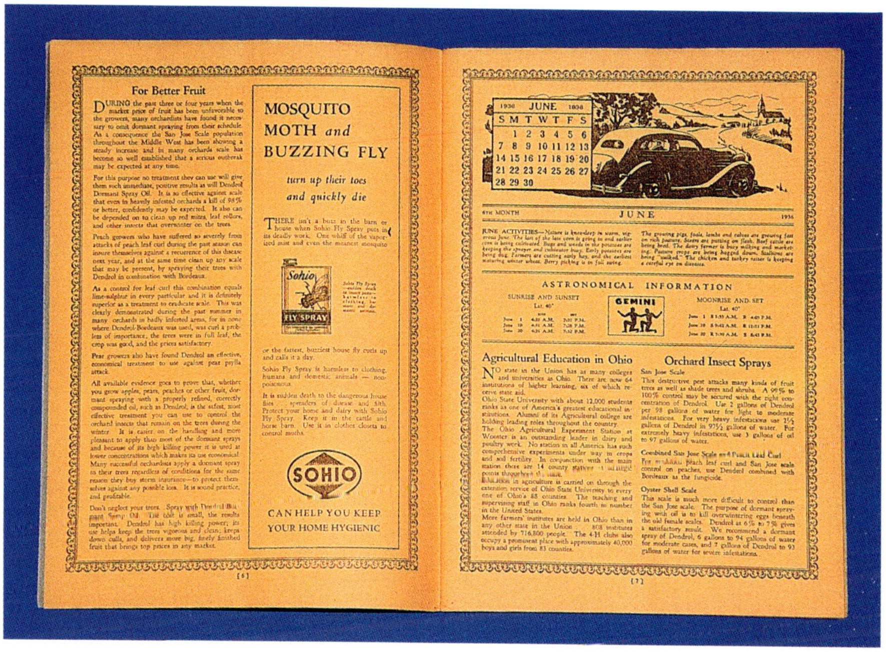

Sohio Farm Guide, 1936. $15-25

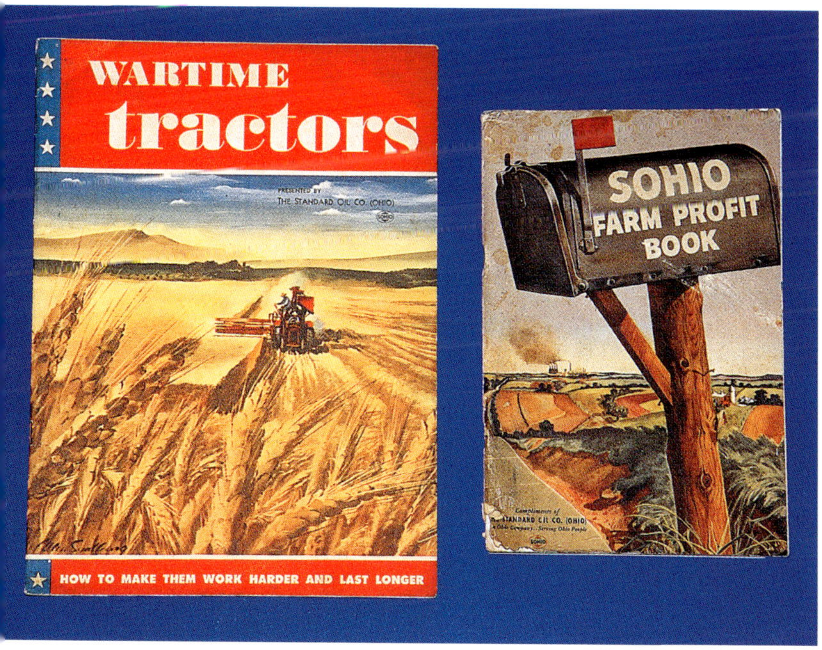

Wartime Tractor Service, 1943, $10-20. Sohio Farm Profit Book, 1946, $25-35.

Sohio Farm Books, 1955-1959. $15-25 each

Farm Guides: 1951, 1952, 1954, 1955, 1956. $15-25 each

Sohio Farm Books, original artwork, 1960. $50 each

Sohio Rain Gauge, 1957. $35-65

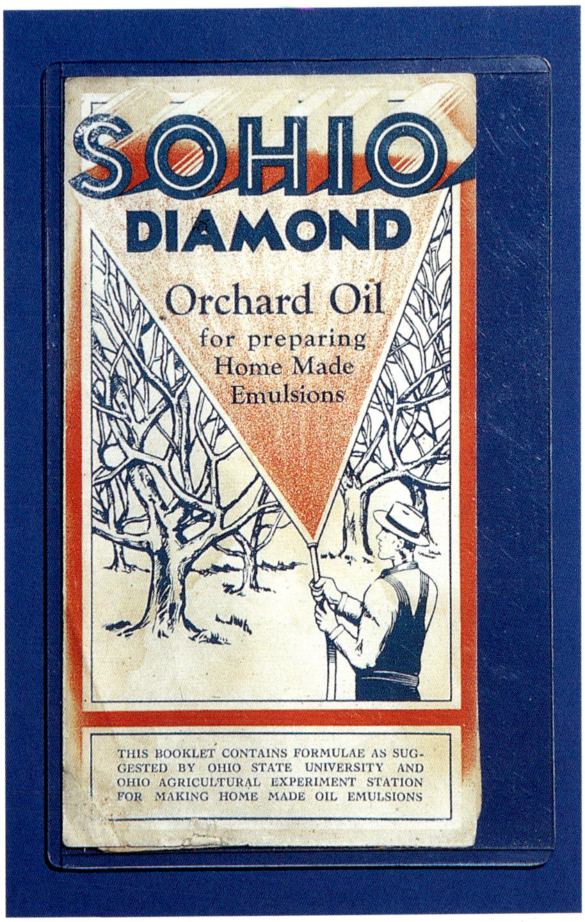

Sohio Orchard Oil leaflet, 1935. $15-25

Sohio Insecticide cans shipping box, 1935. $25-45

Commercial & Industrial
Motor Oils

Left: Sohio Octron HD, 1-quart can, 1962-1964, $25-35 (S1 oil).
Right: Sohio Octron HD, 1-quart can, 1964-1965, $25-35.

Sohio Multron, 1-quart can. Left: May 1966-1965, $15-25.
Right: 1975, $10-20

Left: Sohio Cetron HD, 1-quart can, 1964-1968, $25-35 (S3 oil).
Right: Sohio CHD, 1-quart can, 1965-1966, $35-45.

Sohio Nitron, 1-quart can. Left: May 1966-1975, $15-25.
Right: 1975, $10-20.

Sohio Facto, 1-quart can. Left: 1966-1969, $15-25.
Right: 1969-1975, $15-25.

Left: Sohio Facto, 1-quart can, 1975, $10-20.
Right: Sohio Facto Supreme, 1-quart can, 1975, $10-20.

Lubricants

Sohio Products, 5-gallon can, 1946. $25-45.

Sohio Transformer Oil, 1-gallon can, 1949. $25-45

SOHICYL 650, 5-gallon can, 1954. $25-35

Left: SOHIVIS #57, 5 gallon can, 1958, $25-35.
Right: SOHISPIN Spindle Oil 5 gallon can, 1958, $25-35.

SohioSpin Spindle Oil, 1-gallon can, 1962-1964. $20-30

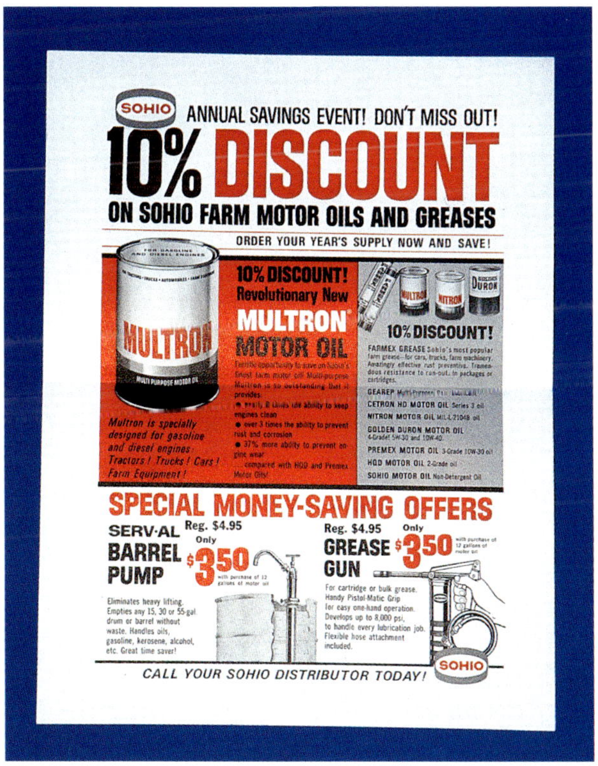

Sohio farm oil deal mailer, 1967. Sent to farmers and commercial accounts at the beginning of the season. $5-10

Sohio product sample or lab use cans, 1-quart, 1957. $20-30 each

Sohio drum decals, 1953-1973. $5-20 each

ALL SEASON MOTOR OIL
GOLDEN
DURON
4-GRADE
SAE 5W-30
RUST PROOFING COMPOUND
SUPER 7C's MULTI-DUTY
OUTBOARD MOTOR OIL
SIXTY TWO
MOTOR OIL
SAE 10W30
A QUALITY MOTOR OIL FOR 1962 MODEL CARS AND OLDER
NOT RECOMMENDED FOR CARS EQUIPPED WITH EMISSION CONTROL SYSTEMS (PCV)
HD
CETRON
MOTOR OIL

NITREX
5W-40
MOTOR OIL
GOLDEN DURON
185 V.I.
MOTOR OIL
OCTRON HD
MOTOR OIL
AUTOMATIC TRANSMISSION FLUID
TYPE F
INDUSTRIAL - MINING - CONSTRUCTION - EARTH MOVING - TRANSPORTATION EQUIPMENT
GEAREP
SPECIAL PURPOSE LUBRICANT

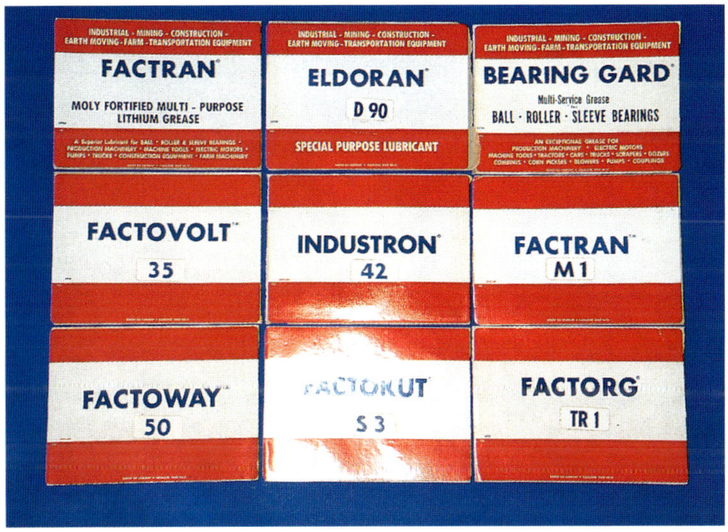
INDUSTRIAL - MINING - CONSTRUCTION - EARTH MOVING - FARM - TRANSPORTATION EQUIPMENT
FACTRAN
MOLY FORTIFIED MULTI - PURPOSE LITHIUM GREASE
INDUSTRIAL - MINING - CONSTRUCTION - EARTH MOVING - TRANSPORTATION EQUIPMENT
ELDORAN
D 90
SPECIAL PURPOSE LUBRICANT
INDUSTRIAL - MINING - CONSTRUCTION - EARTH MOVING - FARM - TRANSPORTATION EQUIPMENT
BEARING GARD
Multi-Service Grease
BALL - ROLLER - SLEEVE BEARINGS
FACTOVOLT
35
INDUSTRON
42
FACTRAN
M1
FACTOWAY
50
S 3
FACTORG
TR 1

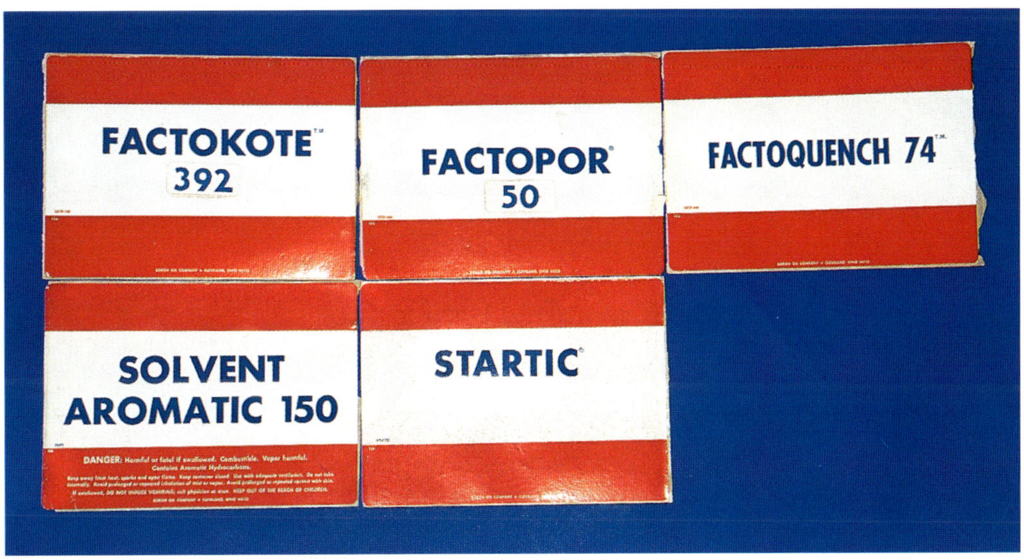
FACTOKOTE
392
FACTOPOR
50
FACTOQUENCH 74
SOLVENT
AROMATIC 150
DANGER: Harmful or fatal if swallowed. Combustible. Vapor harmful.
STARTIC

Sohio Heat

The Sohio Heat Division sold fuel, oil, oil burner service and fuel fired products to residential, commercial and industrial customers.

Left: Sohio Heat salesman's book, 1963, $25-35.
Right: Sohio Heat receipt folder, 1963, $10-20

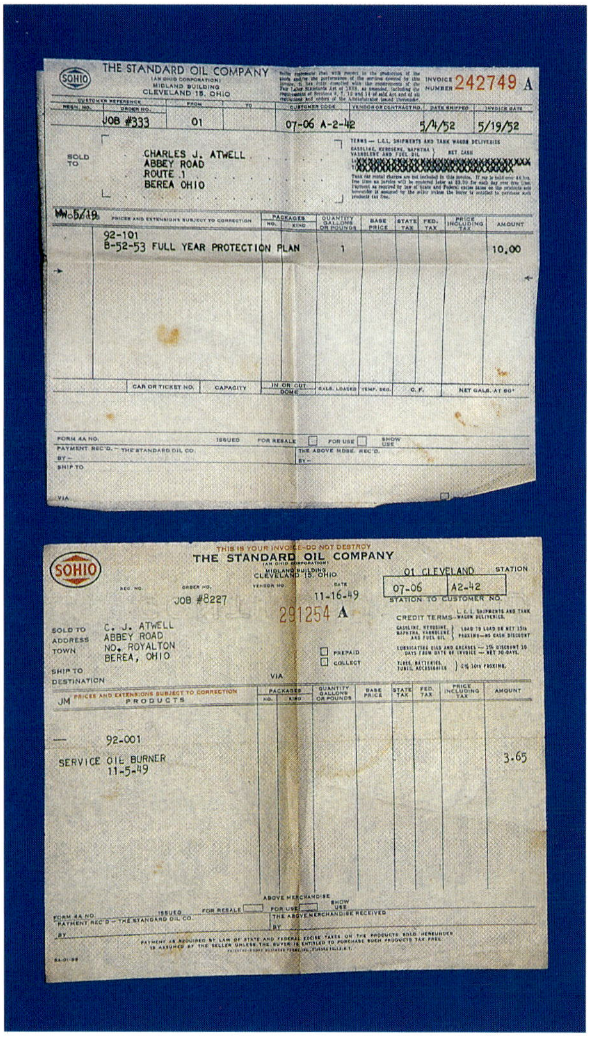

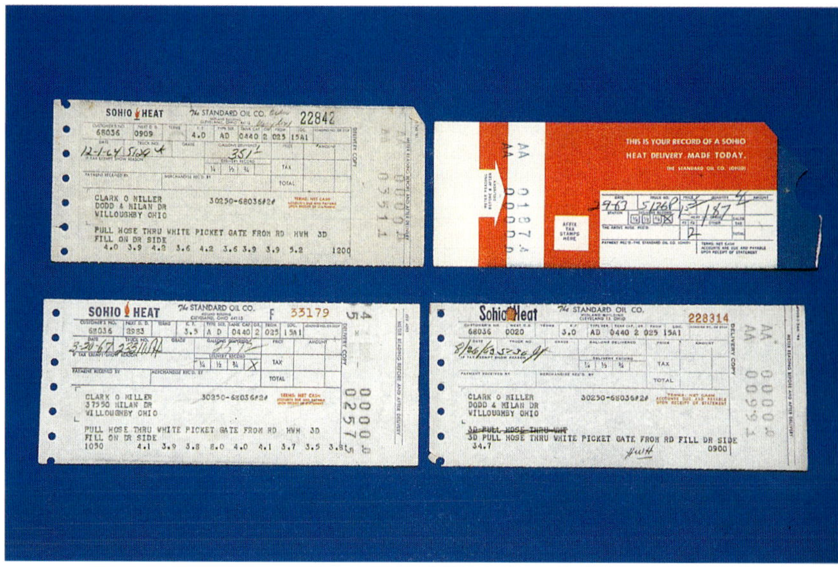

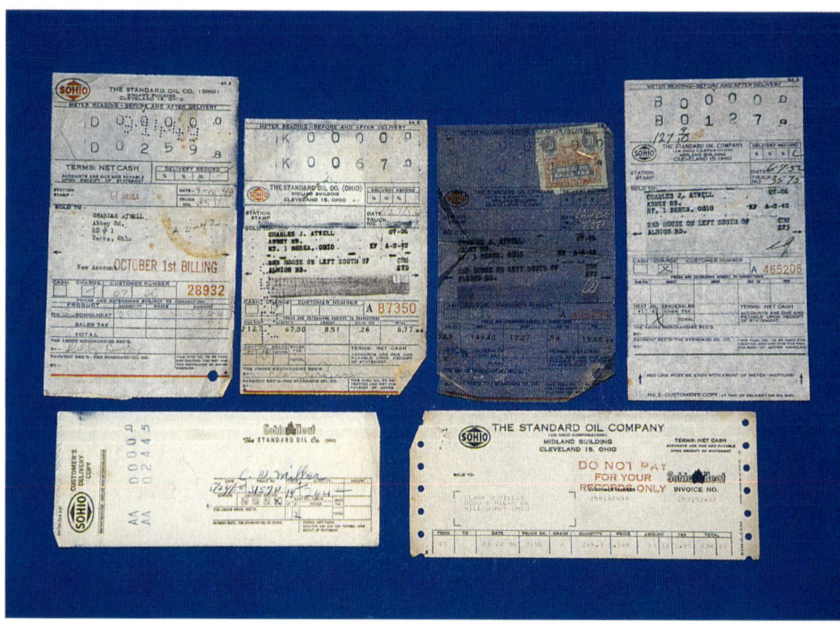

Sohio Heat delivery receipts, 1948-1965. $5-10 each

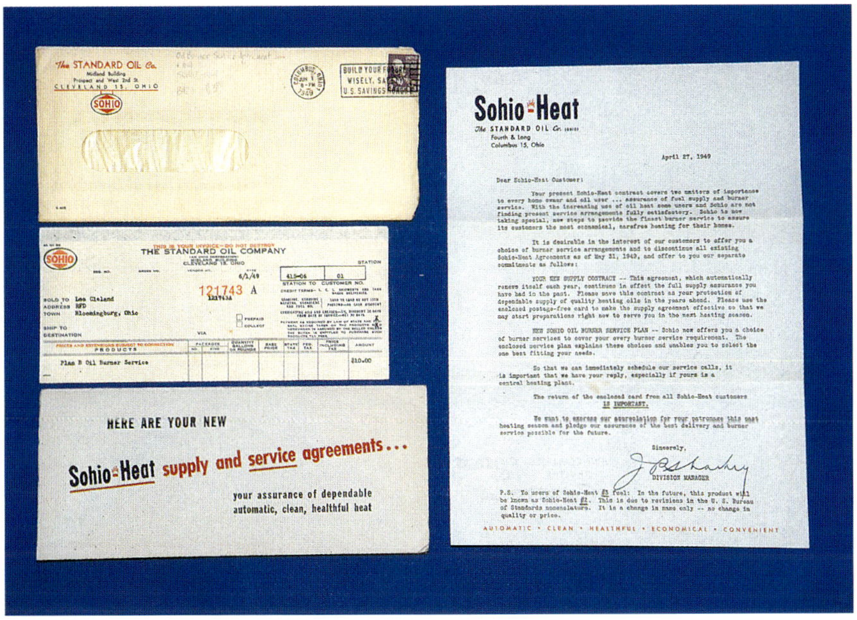

Sohio Heat yearly contract, 1948. $10-20

Oil Fired Equipment catalog, 1962. $15-20

How to Save Money on Heating Oil book, 1959. $10-15

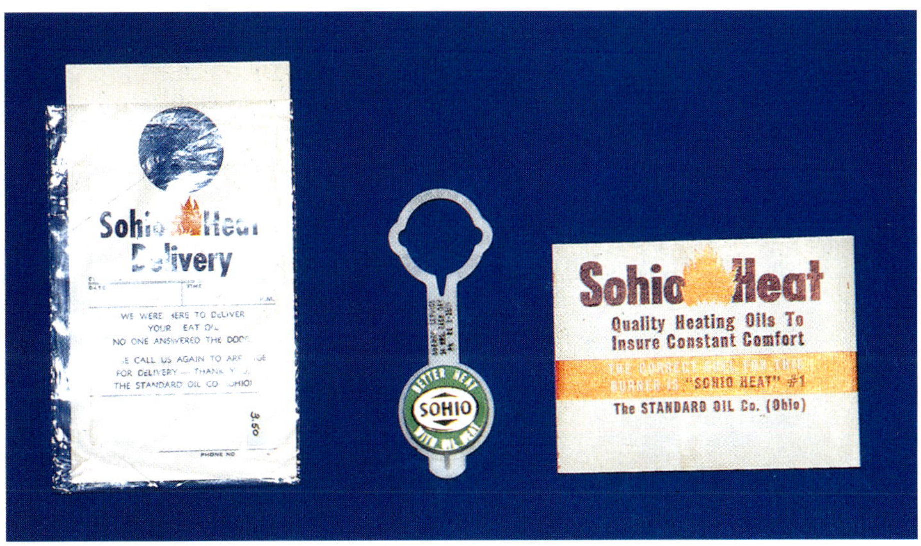

Sohio Heat delivery notice, giveaway bottle cap, furnace sticker, 1956-1966. $5-10 each

Chapter Four
Other Consumer Items

Maps and Map Racks

Sohio Road Maps, 1928-1937. $25-50 each.

Sohio Road Maps, 1938-1941. $15-25 each.

Sohio 1939 World's Fair route map, rare. $35-65

Sohio road maps, 1942-1946. $15-20 each

Sohio road maps, 1950-1963, $10-15 each

Sohio road maps, 1969-1979. $5-8 each

Sohio road maps, 1963-1967, 1949, 1953, 1961, Eastern & US, $10-12

Left: Sohio Tour Guide, 1934, $15-25. Right: Sohio Tour Guide, 1941, $15-25.

Sohio Tour Guide, 1934, inside fold.

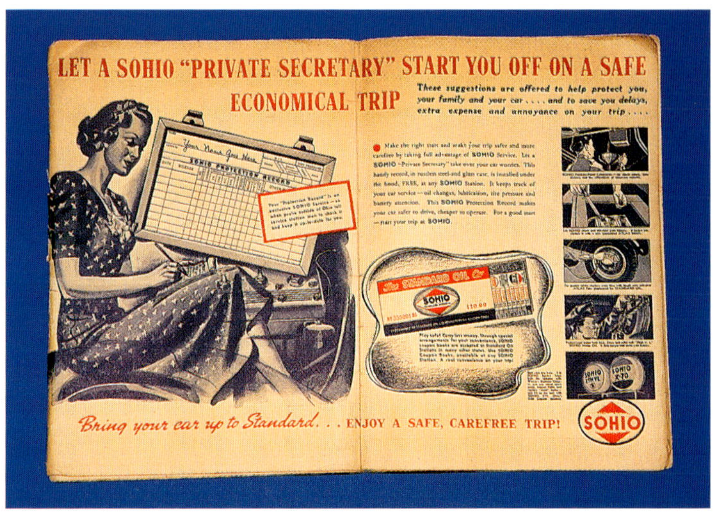

Sohio Tour Guide, 1941, inside fold.

Sohio Tour Guides, 1955-1963. $5-15 each

Sohio street guides, 1961, 1962, 1964, 1972. $5-10 each

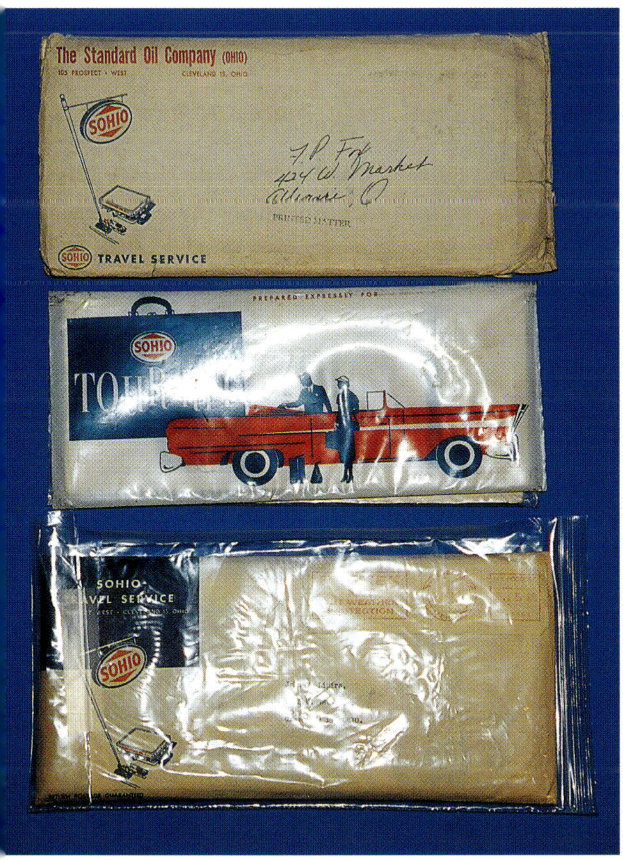

Sohio Tour Guides, 1958-1960. $10-25 each

Sohio Street Guides, 1940, 1957, 1959. $10-15 each

Sohio travel logs, 1958, 1961. $10-15 each. Sohio car record book with envelope, 1952, $10-20.

Sohio Ohio Tour Guides, 1926-1963. $10-20

Pictorial Ohio Guide, 1933. $15-30

Sohio Tour Guide 1926, reverse side.

Left: Sohio Cruise Guide, 1966, $5-7.
Right: Sohio Marine Information, 1959, $10-20.

Sohio map rack, 1960. As shown, $225-425.

Sohio picnic area guide, 1949. $5-15

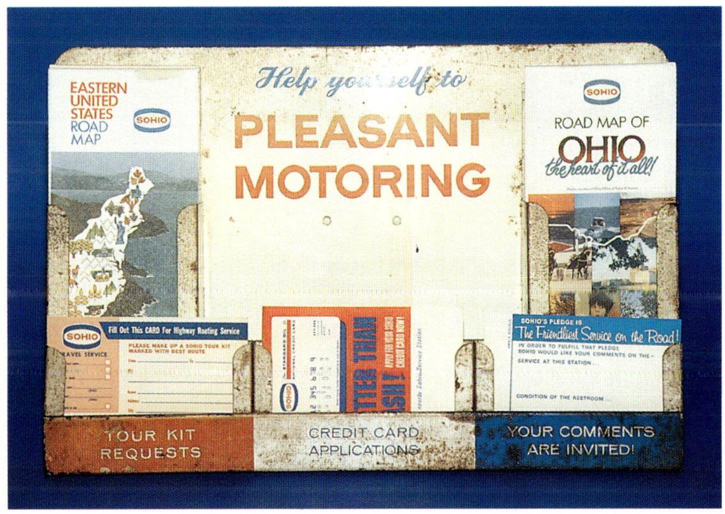

Sohio map rack, 1965. As shown, $200-325.

Sohio map rack, 1962. As shown, $225-375.

Toledo Refinery Guide Book with experimental logo, 1958.
$15-25

Calendars

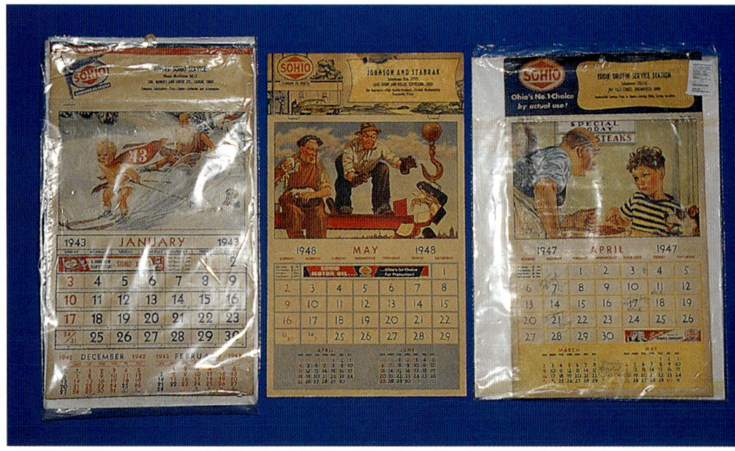

Sohio calendars, 1943, 1948, 1947. $35-50 each

Sohio calendars, 1938 and 1941. $35-50 each

Sohio calendars, 1957 and 1962. $25-35 each

Sohio calendars, 1949 and 1945. $35-50 each

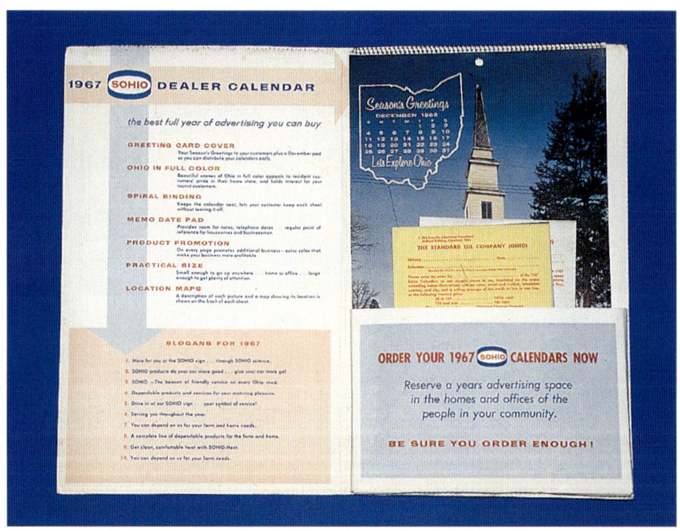

Sohio Dealer calendar order packet, 1967. $15-30

Sohio calendars given by distributors, 1962, $15-25. 1977, $10-20.

Sohio calendars, 1963, 1966, 1964. $15-35 each

Sohio calendars, 1971, 1976, 1970. $10-20 each

Banks

Sohio glass block bank (front and back), December 1941, 4" x 4". $65-85

Sohio dime bank, 1949. $10-20

Sohio oval plastic bank, 1951. $20-30

Left: Sohio Farmex bank, August 1955, $25-35.
Right: Sohio Premex bank, 1955, $15-30.

Credit Cards

Sohio credit cards and mailers, 1953-1989. $15-75 each

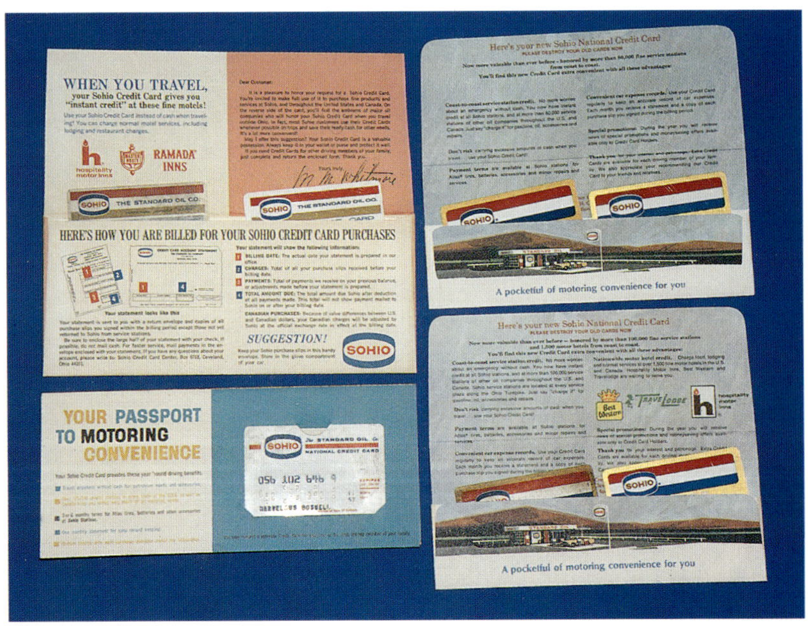

NATIONAL CREDIT CARD
Frank Valentine
2812 E. Wallings Road
Brecksville, Ohio
The STANDARD SOHIO OIL Co. (OHIO)
NATIONAL CREDIT CARD
The STANDARD OIL Co.
AN OHIO CORPORATION
EXPIRES: MARCH 31, 1953
Mary Louise Upham
R. F. D. 2
Willoughby, Ohio
SOHIO
NATIONAL CREDIT CARD
The STANDARD SOHIO OIL Co. (OHIO)
EXPIRES: DECEMBER 31, 1957
032 259 087 8
MRS CARL WEYER
829 PUTNAM ST
FINDLAY OHIO
The STANDARD OIL Co.
NATIONAL CREDIT CARD
032 259 087 8
MRS CARL WEYER
829 PUTNAM ST
FINDLAY OHIO
The STANDARD OIL Co.
NATIONAL CREDIT CARD
025 257 042 9
FRANK VALENTINE
The STANDARD OIL Co.
NATIONAL CREDIT CARD
025 257 042 9
FRANK VALENTINE
SOHIO The STANDARD OIL Co.
NATIONAL CREDIT CARD
025 257 042 9
FRANK VALENTINE
SOHIO The STANDARD OIL Co.
NATIONAL CREDIT CARD
025 257 042 9
FRANK VALENTINE

SOHIO The STANDARD OIL Co.
NATIONAL CREDIT CARD
032 259 087 8
MRS CARL WEYER
SOHIO The STANDARD OIL Co.
NATIONAL CREDIT CARD
027 163 990 8
CARL GORBACH
SOHIO The STANDARD OIL Co.
NATIONAL CREDIT CARD
032 259 087 8
MRS CARL WEYER
SOHIO The STANDARD OIL Co.
NATIONAL CREDIT CARD
025 257 042 9
FRANK VALENTINE
MALCO SAMPLE
SOHIO The STANDARD OIL Co.
NATIONAL CREDIT CARD
025 257 042 9
FRANK VALENTINE
SOHIO
NATIONAL CARD
025 257 042 9
FRANK VALENTINE
SOHIO THE STANDARD OIL CO.
NATIONAL CREDIT CARD
025 257 042 9
FRANK VALENTINE

SOHIO THE STANDARD OIL CO.
025 305 472 0
SOHIO THE STANDARD OIL CO.
025 257 042 9
SOHIO
THE STANDARD OIL CO.
025 257 042 9
FRANK VALENTINE
SOHIO
THE STANDARD OIL CO.
025 257 042 9
FRANK VALENTINE
SOHIO
THE STANDARD OIL CO.
025 257 042 9
FRANK VALENTINE
025 257 042 9
FRANK VALENTINE
SOHIO
025 257 042 9
FRANK VALENTINE
025 257 042 9
FRANK VALENTINE

SOHIO
025 217 990 8 00002
CLARK C MILLER
BP
025 217 990 8 00001
BORON BORON OIL COMPANY
NATIONAL CREDIT
038 200 797 9
RICHARD STOLTENBURG
BORON
BORON OIL COMPANY
038 446 724 7
JOHN R KNOX

Thermometers

Sohio Guaranteed Starting thermometer (with box), 1954. $75-125

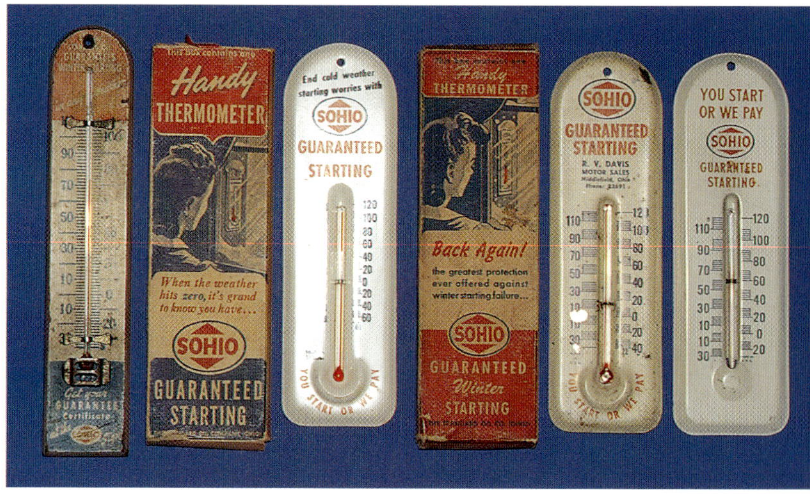

Sohio Guaranteed Starting Thermometer, 10" long, 1943, 1947, 1954, 1957. $45-95 each

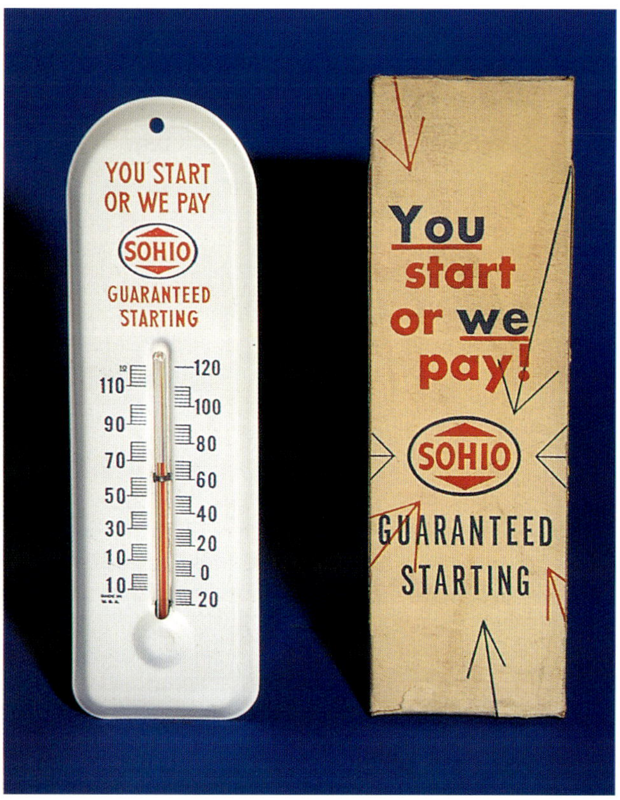

Sohio Guaranteed Starting Thermometer, 1956. $50-100, with box.

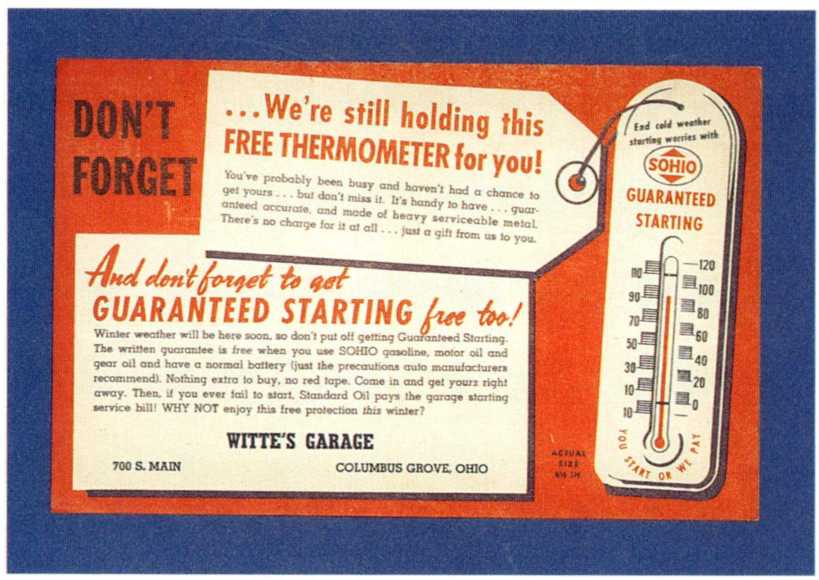

Sohio Guaranteed Starting Thermometer Mailer, 1947. $20-30

Sohio Boron thermometer, 12" diameter, 1956. $250-350

Super Sohio thermometer, 12" diameter, 1938. $250-500

Sohio distributor thermometer and oven rack tool, 1970-1980. $15-45

Sohio Guaranteed Starting Thermometer, 8 1/2" x 38 1/2", 1954. $200-400

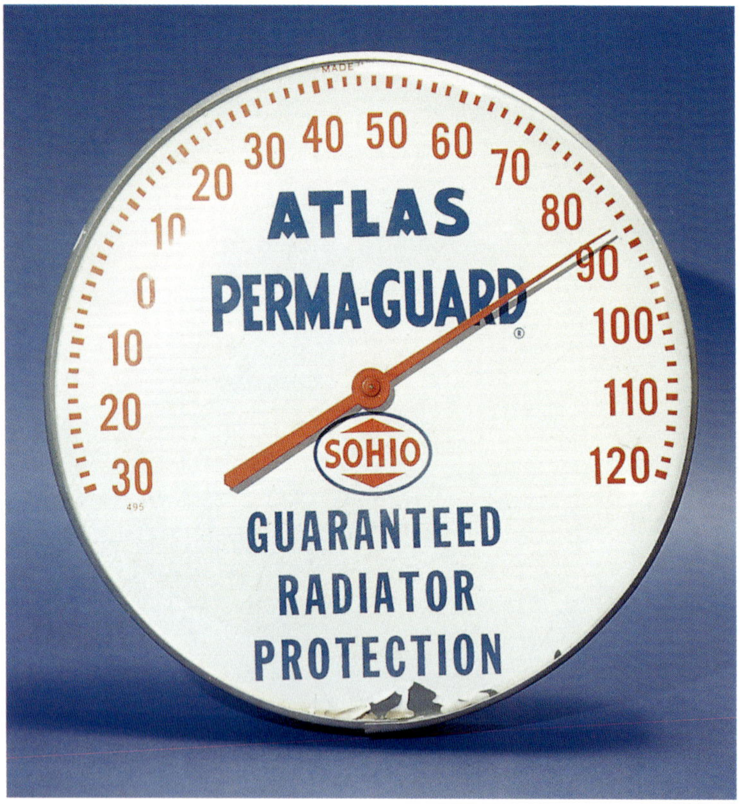

Sohio GRP thermometer, 12" diameter, 1960. $250-350

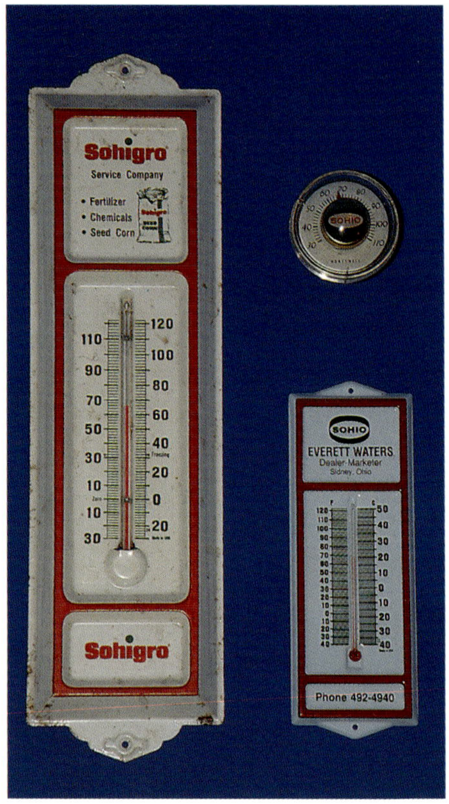

Sohio thermometers, 1962-1972. $50-75 each

Salt & Pepper Shakers

Sohio salt & pepper shakers, 1948. $250-350

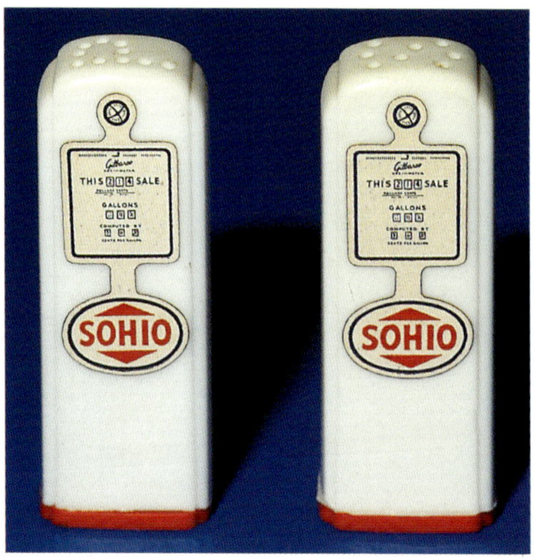

Sohio salt & pepper shakers, 1955. $250-300

Sohio salt & pepper shakers, 1961. $75-125

Give-Away Items

Sohio Boron/Premex shopping bags, both sides printed, 1958. $10-20

Sohio shopping bag, Extron gasoline, 1958. $10-20

Reverse side of Extron Gasoline shopping bag, HQD Motor Oil.

Sohio Heat/Duron shopping bag, 1963. $10-20

Sohio shopping bag, 1966. $10-20

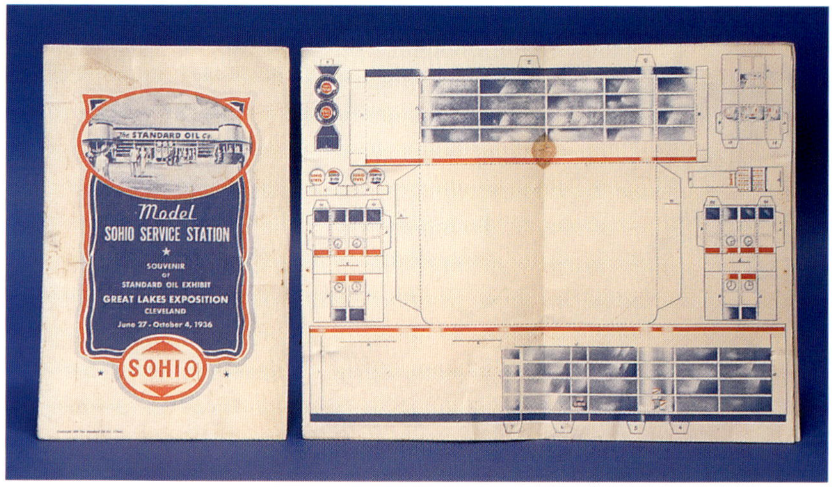

Sohio paper service station give-away for Great Lakes Exposition, 1936. $75-150

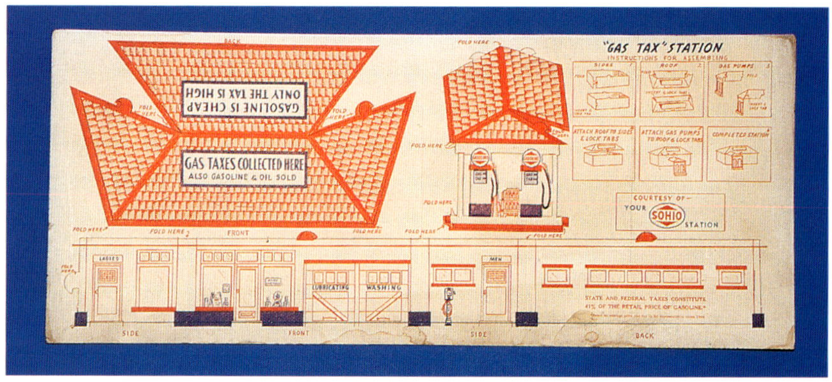

Sohio "Gas Tax" toy service station, paper, 1949. $25-35

Sohio playing cards, 1950-1960. $15-45

Sohio playing cards, 1944, 1962-1972. $10-30 each

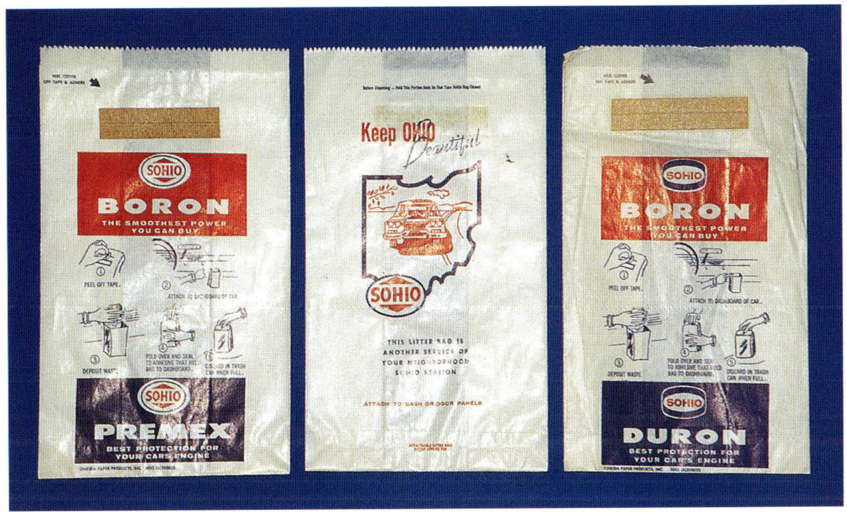

Sohio litter bags, 1960 and 1962. $5-8 each

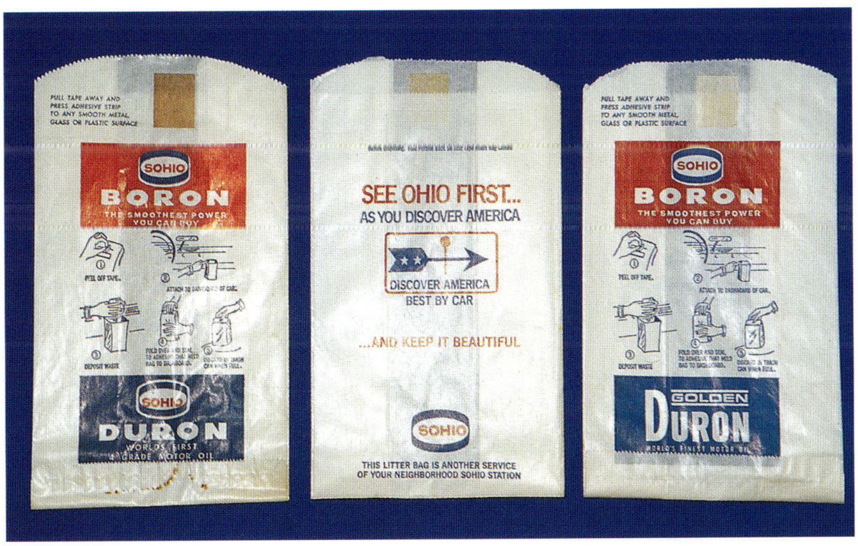

Sohio litter bags, 1963 and 1965. $5-8 each

Sohio Hayride Gang radio show songbook, 1940. $15-25

Sohio jigsaw puzzles, 1934-1938. $25-45 each

Sohio gas ration stamp books, 1943, $10-25. Center: Sohio Moto-Record book, 1943, $10-30.

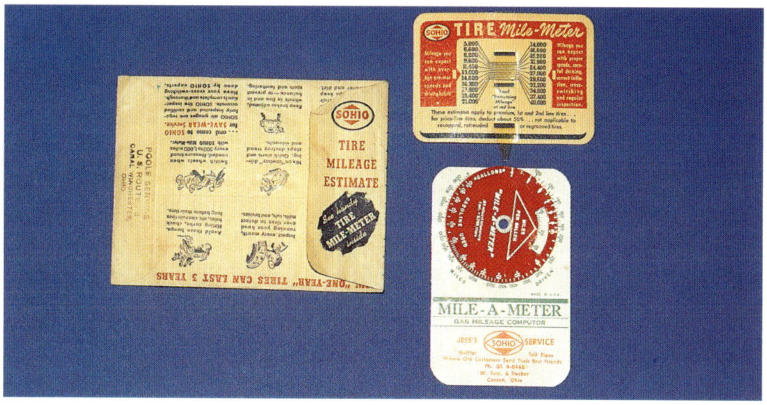

Sohio Tire Mile-Meter, 1943, $25-35. Sohio Mile-A-Meter, 1940, $10-15.

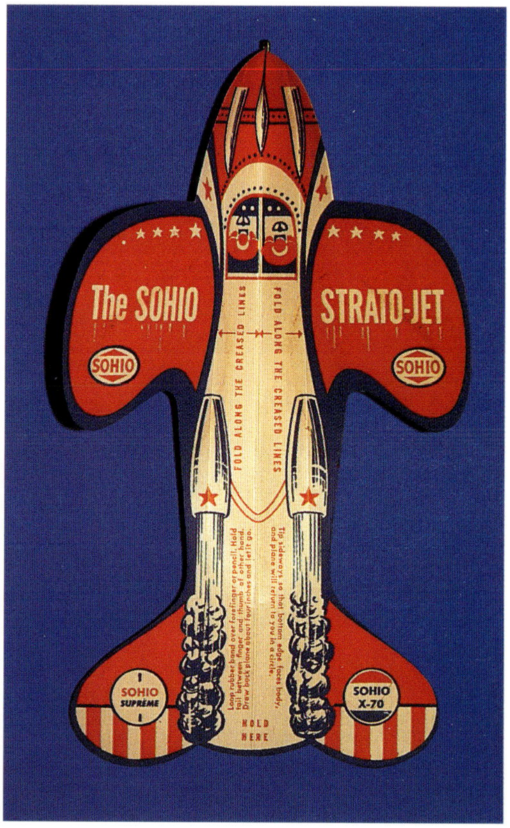

Sohio Strato-Jet toy airplane, 1949. $15-30

Ohio sales tax exempt card, 1945, $5-10. Sohio ink blotters, 1930, 1940, 1950. $15-35 each

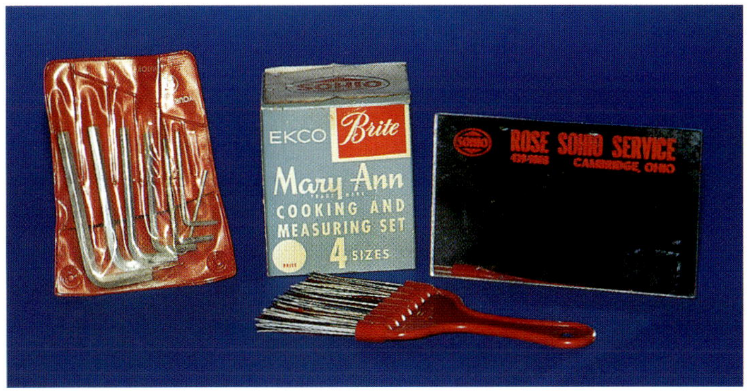

Various Sohio customer direct mail items, 1940-1950, $15-25. National Air Race envelope with ticket stubs, 1947, $25-35.

Sohio dealer giveaways, 1950-1962. $20-30 each

Sohio plastic toy tank truck, sold at Sohio stations at Christmas, 1960. Could be filled with water. $125-225

Sohio dealer give-aways, 1950-1962. $25-100 each

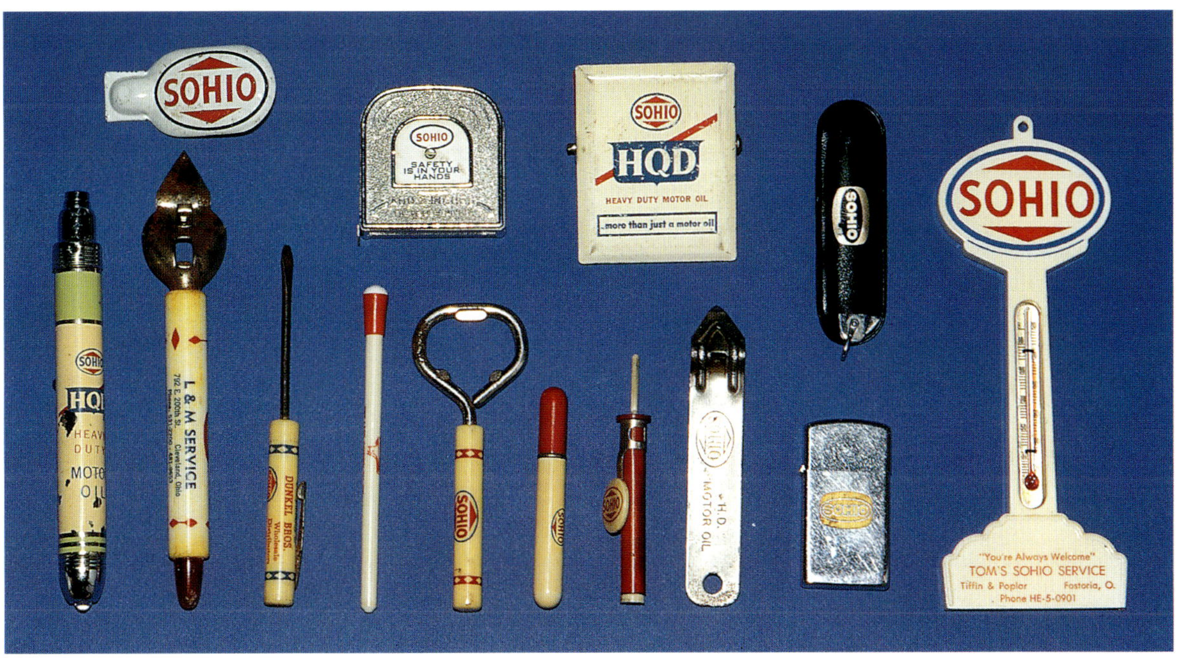

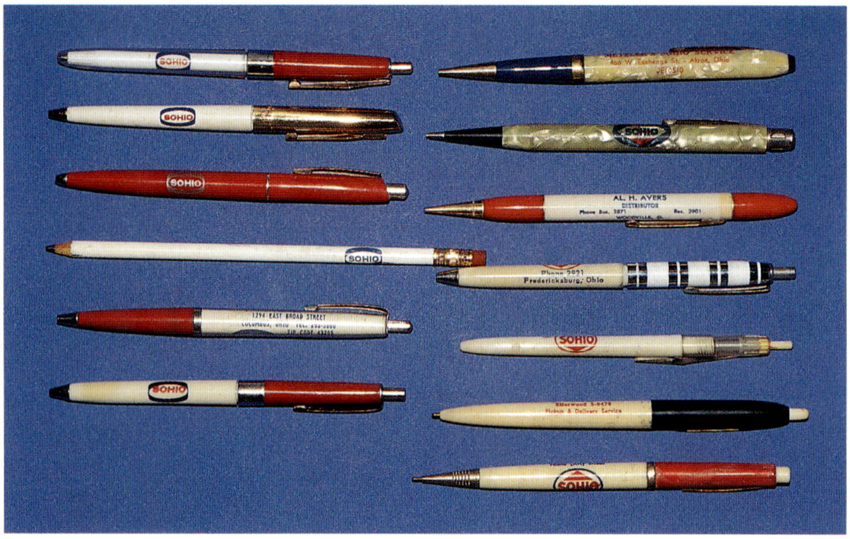

Sohio pens and pencils, 1930-1970. $5-50 each

Sohio keys and key chains, 1945 and 1965. $25-45 each

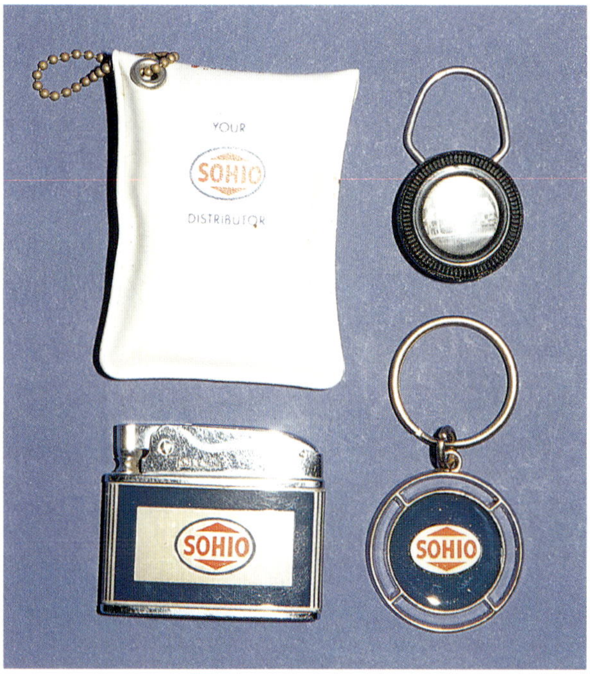

Sohio key tags, rain bonnet, and lighter, 1955-1962. $10-50 each

Sohio key tags, coin purses, golf ball marker, 1962-1969. $20-30 each

Sohio postcards, 1959. $1-5 each

Sohio X70 window coat hook, 1938. $45-60

Future Farmers of America pinback, courtesy of Standard Oil of Ohio, 1945. $35-50

Sohio matchbooks, 1935-1965. $5-10 each

Sohio pocket knife, 3 1/4" long, 1955-1962. $25-35

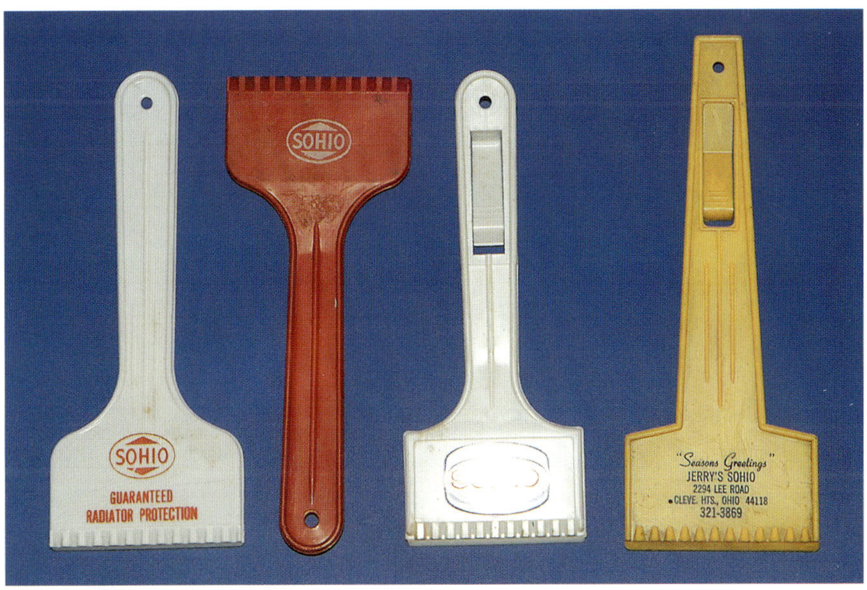

Sohio ice scrapers, 1955 thru 1965. $10-20 each

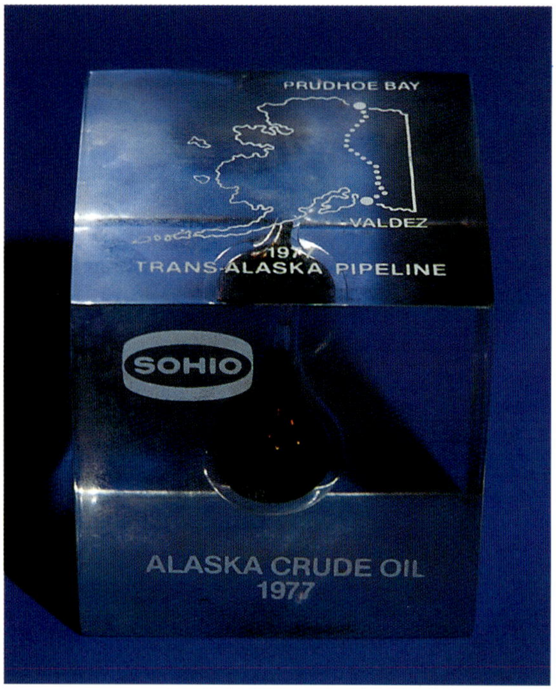

Sohio Alaska crude oil paperweight, 1977. $25-30

Sohio plastic cups, 1980-1990. $5-8 each

Sohio wall clock, giveaway for opening day of a new station, showing both logos, 1962. $74-95. This design has come up recently on two other clocks and a thermos;this may be a fantasy piece.

Public service awards, given by Sohio to a radio station, 1948-1949 and 1950-1951. $5-15 each

Sohio drinking glasses, 1980-1990. $10-15 each

Sohio/Cleveland Browns antenna flag, 1976. $5-10

Aviation Items

Program for Cleveland Ohio Air Races, 1932. Artwork for cover painted by father of Sohio collector Roger Hubbell. $100-300

Program for Cleveland Ohio Air Races, 1935. $125-200

Program for Cleveland Ohio Air Races, 1937. $100-175

Sohio Aircraft Log (front).

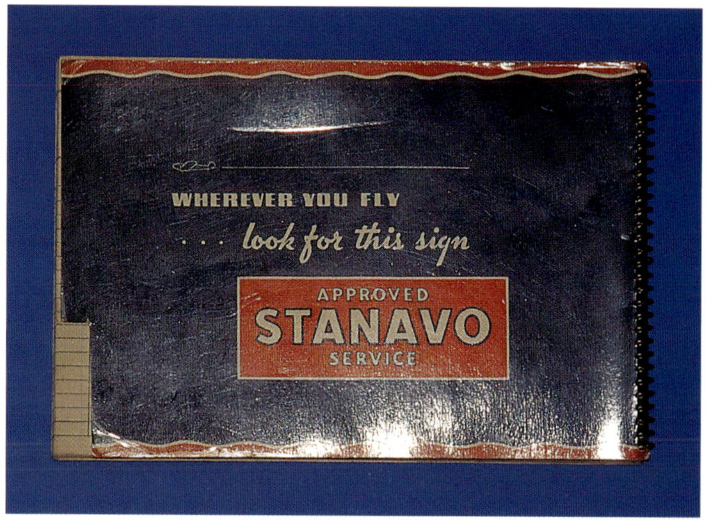

Sohio Aircraft Pilot's Log (reverse), 1936. $30-50. Stanavo was Esso's brand of aviation products.

Sohio airport windsock, 1958. $250-500

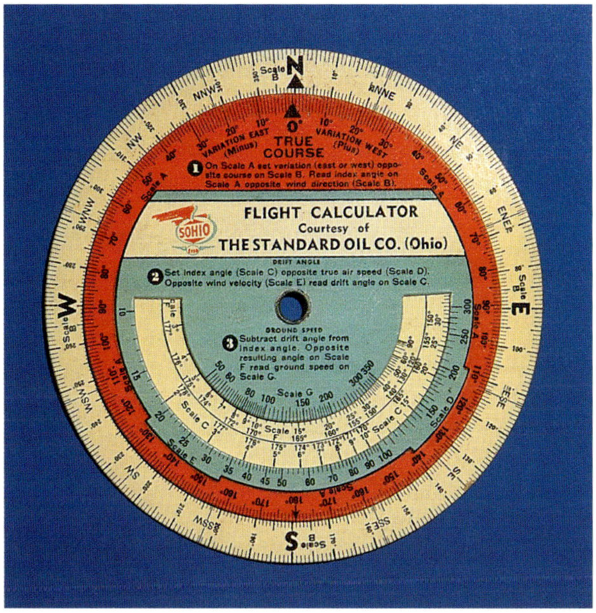

Sohio Aviation slide rule, 1954. $20-40

RPM Aviation Oil, 1-quart cans. 1961, $25-30 each. 1975, $15-25. RPM was Chevron's brand of oils.

RPM Aviation Oil, 1-quart can, 1959. $25-35 each

Sohio Aviation slide rule, 1962 and 1959, $25-35 each.
Center: Sohio-Giro aircraft book, 1931, $25-50.

Chapter Five
Station & Company-Related Items

Gas Pumps and Globes

Late 1950s Sohio pumps, Mt. Gilead, Ohio, August 1969.

Sohio Marine globe, three pieces, glass, 1955. $900-1,250. *From the Scott Benjamin collection.*

Sohio Heat pump globe, three pieces, glass, 1946-1954. $500-750. *From the Scott Benjamin collection.*

Sohio station, Cleveland, Ohio, 1938.

Red Crown pump globe with green border. three pieces, 13 1/2-inch metal body, 1928-1930. $1,350-1,800.

Red Crown pump globe with blue border. three pieces, 13 1/2-inch metal body, 1928-1930. $1,350-1,850

Sohio Supreme pump globe, three pieces, glass, 1940. $400-650. This globe is being reproduced.

Sohio X70 pump globe, three pieces, glass, 1940. $400-600

Renown pump lens, 1933-1946. $200-225, lens only. $400-650, complete globe.

Sohio Xtane pump globe, three pieces, glass, 1951. $400-600

Boron Supreme pump globe, three pieces, glass body, 1956. $350-450

Sohio Extron pump globe, three pieces, glass, 1957. $350-450

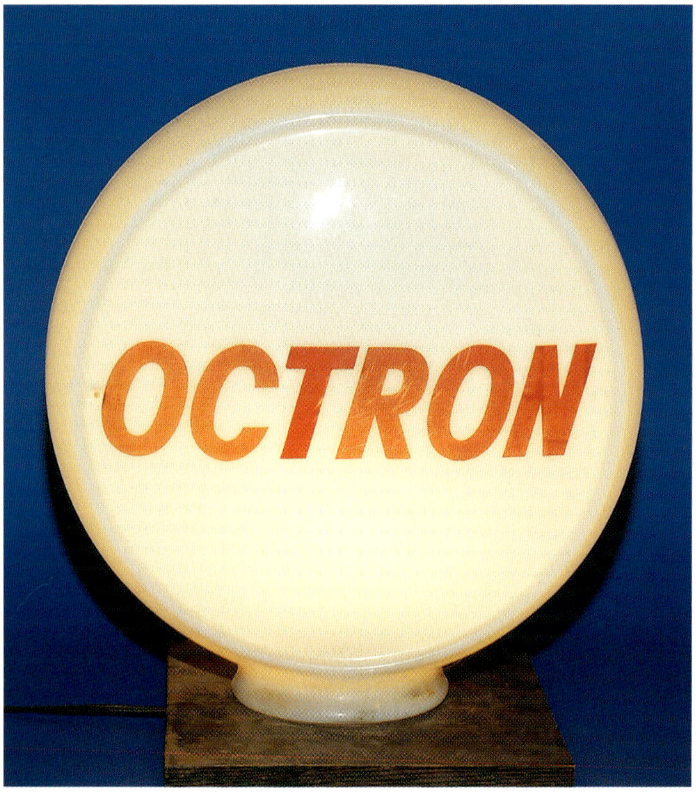

Sohio Octron globe—globe body with Octron stick-on letters, 1964-1968. $300-475

Sohio Diesel pump globe, three pieces, glass, 1948-1955. $450-650

Sohio Diesel pump globe, three pieces, glass, 1946-1954. $400-650

Sohio Diesel Supreme pump globe, three pieces, glass, April 1962-1967. $250-375

Sohio Premix Outboard gas pump globe, three pieces, glass, 1946-1958. $1,000-1,500

Sohio Extron Marine, three pieces, glass, 1957. $600-900

Sohio Kerosene pump globe, three pieces, glass, 1946-1954. $400-600

Sohio Aviation pump globe, three pieces, glass, 1946-1954. $800-1,200

Sohio glass pump inserts, 1965-1973. $10-25 each

Sohio Plastic Pump Inserts, 1973-1989. $5-10 each

Sohio pump/lubester decals, 1962-1972. $5-15 each

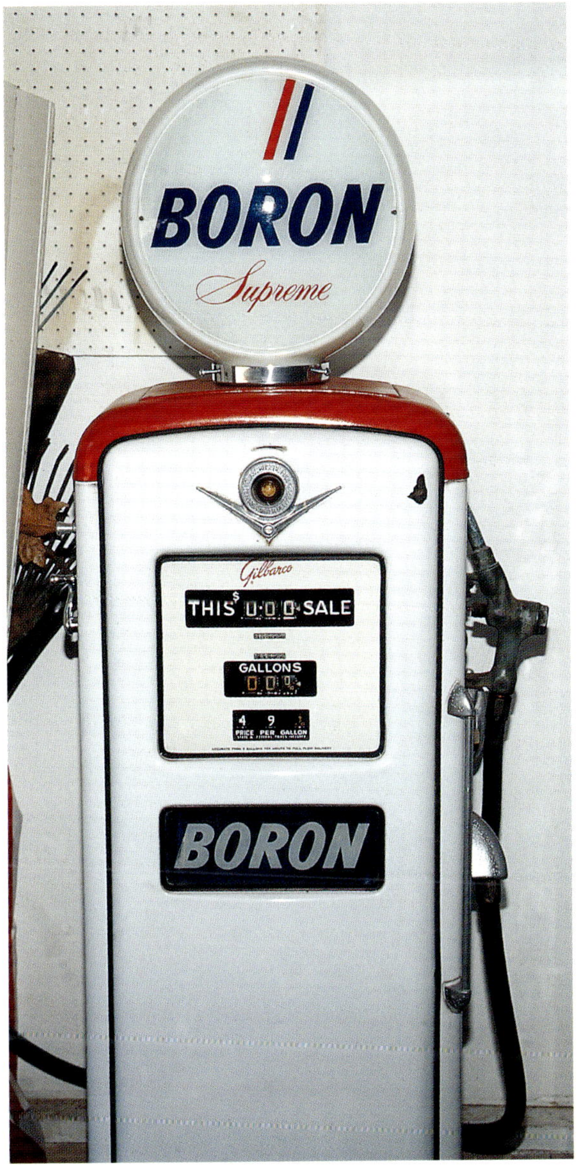

Sohio Boron gas pump with globe, Tokheim Calco Meter, 1954. $1,000-1,300

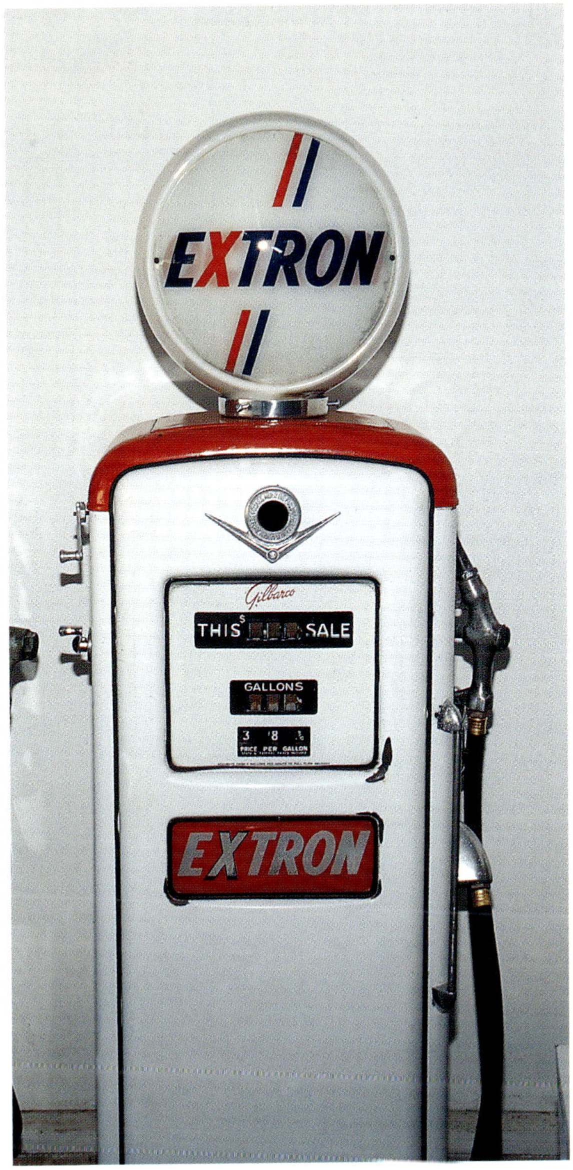

Sohio Extron gas pump with globe, Tokheim Calco Meter, 1954. $1,000-1,300

Globe List

The following is a list of all known pump globes from Sohio and their affiliates. Like other companies, they used a variety of stylesover the years. A special thank-you to Scott Benjamin and Wayne Henderson for their expertise in this field of collecting.

Globe	Years	Value
Red Crown Gasoline (RW-white with no border)	1912-1920	$3,000-4000
Red Crown Gasoline (RW-white with border)	1917-1924	$3,000-4,000
Red Crown Gasoline (Metal HP Red)	1920-1926	$950-1,400
Red Crown Gasoline (15" Metal HP Red)	1926-1930	$1,500-2,000
Red Crown Ethyl Gasoline (15" Metal HP RED)	1926-1928	$700-1,000
Red Crown Gasoline (15" Metal HP Red)	1928-1930	$1,400-1,800
Red Crown Gasoline (13.5" Glass W)	1928-1930	$850-1,250
Sohio Ethyl Gasoline (13.5" Metal HP Red)	1928-1934	$900-1,350
Sohio Ethyl Gasoline (13.5" Glass W)	1928-1934	$700-1,000
Sohio X-70 (15" Metal Hp Red)	1930-1934	$700-1,000
Sohio X-70 (13.5" Glass W)	1930-1950	$350-550
Sohio Motor Oil (15" Metal HP Red)	1930-1934	$800-1,200
Sohio Motor Oil (13.5" Glass W)	1934-1940	$700-1,000
Sohio Ethyl (13.5" Glass W)	1934-1939	$300-500
Renown Green (13.5" Glass W)	1930-1934	$300-500
Renown (13.5" Glass W)	1934-1946	$250-450
Sohio X-Tane (13.5" Glass W)	1940-1958	$350-550
Sohio Supreme (13.5" Glass W)	1939-1954	$300-500
Sohio Kerosene (13.5" Glass)	1940-1970	$250-400
Kerosene (13.5" Glass W)	1950s	$200-325
Sohio Diesel Red/White/Blue 5 (13.5" Glass W)	1946-1950	$450-650
Sohio Diesel (13.5" Glass W)	1950-1970	$250-400
Diesel Supreme (13.5" Glass W)	1950s	$250-375
Diesel Supreme (15" Metal)	1950s	No listing
Sohio Aviation (13.5" Glass W)	1946-1970	$600-900
Sohio Aviation (13.5" Glass W)	1946-1970	$600-900
Sohio Heat (13.5" Glass W)	1946-1970	$400-650
Sohio Marine Gasoline (13.5" Glass W)	1946-1954	$700-950
Sohio Pre-Mixed Outboard (13.5" Glass W)	1946-1958	$1,000-1,500
Boron Supreme (13.5" Glass W)	1954-1962	$250-350
Extron (13.5" Glass W)	1958-1962	$250-350
Octron (13.5" Glass W)	1960s-1980s	$125-225
Boron Marine (13.5" Glass W)	1954-1962	$450-750
Extron Marine (13.5" Glass W)	1958-1962	$500-800
Hi-So (Green Glass 13-1/2")	1931-1933	
(Sohio Power Fuel for Distillate Tractors, Type not known, 1946)		
Sohio Motor Oil (Metal body 15")	1930s	$1,500-2,000
Sohio Motor Oil (Glass Body 13-1/2")	1940s	$1,000-1,500
(These were used on top of the oil bottle cabinet on the island.)		

The Refiners Oil Company
Dayton, Ohio

This Dayton, Ohio based marketer operated around 300 retail stations in Ohio and Indiana. When the General Motors Chemical Company developed the antiknock additive Tetraethyl Lead in early 1923, Dayton based Refiners was chosen to test market the new product. The test was so successful that in September of that year Standard Oil of Indiana signed onto be an exclusive distributor of the new additive, "Ethyl", through its marketing territory. Standard Oil of Ohio purchased Refiners Oil Company in 1930 and re-branded the stations in Ohio to Sohio. A small number of stations in Kentucky and Indiana were sold to Standard Oil Company of Kentucky and remained under the Refiners brand through the early 1930s.

High Speed Filtered Gasoline (OPE)	1915-1920	$1,400-1,800
High Speed Filtered Gasoline (Metal HP)	1915-1920	No Listing
Refiners Gasoline (old car) (15" Metal HP)	1915-1925	No Listing
Refiners Benzol Gasoline (15" Metal HP)	1920-1925	No Listing
Refiners Aero Gas (w/plane) (15" Metal HP)	1920-1925	No Listing
Refiners Ethyl Gasoline (16.5" Metal HP)	1924-1927	$600-950
Refiners Ethyl Gasoline (15" Metal HP)	1924-1927	$600-950
Refiners (orange) (16.5" Metal HP)	1925-1930	$500-800
Refiners (orange) (15" Metal HP)	1925-1930	$500-800
Refiners (orange) (12" Metal HP)	1920s	$900-1,250
Refiners High Test (15" Metal HP)	1928-1930	$600-950
Refiners Ethyl Pioneer Distributors (16" Metal HP)	1927-1930	$900-1,250
Refiners Ethyl Pioneer Distributors (15" Metal HP)	1927-1930	$900-1,250

Canfield Oil Company
Cleveland, Ohio

Founded in Cleveland in 1886, Canfield was primarily a lubricants manufacturer, developing, among others, the "Wm. Penn" motor oils. Canfield became involved in gasoline marketing in the late 1910s, operating stations in and around Cleveland. When Standard Oil purchased Canfield in 1945, there were over 200 branded stations at that time. The Sohio brand name gradually replaced the Canfield name, although Canfield and Wm. Penn motor oils continued in production. In the 1970s, after British Petroleum purchased a controlling interest in Standard Oil, many dealer operated BP station sin the east were re-branded "Wm. Penn", continuing as such until the BP name was selected to replace all Sohio affiliate brand names in 1990.

Canfield Gasoline (15" Metal)	1922-1925	$900-1,250
Wm Penn (15" Metal)	1920s	No Listing
Canfield Gasoline (OPE W)	1920s	No Listing
Canfield Ethyl Gasoline (OPB W)	1920s	No Listing
Canfield (13.5" Glass W)	1930s	$400-700
Canfield Ethyl (EGC) Ethyl (Balcrank)	1930s	$500-800

Caldwell & Taylor
Cincinnati, Ohio

Cincinnati based marketer purchased by Sohio in 1928.

Caldwell & Taylor Original Benzol Gas (OPE RW)	1910s-1920s	$2,500-3,500
Caldwell & Taylor Gas (OPE RW)	1920s	$2,500-3,500
Caldwell & Taylor Original Benzol Gas (15" Metal)	1920s	$900-1,250
Caldwell & Taylor Original Benzol Gas (13.5" Glass)	1927-1928	$750-1,100
Caldwell & Taylor Original Benzol Gas (Balcrank)	1927-1928	$850-1,200

Spears & Riddle
Wheeling, West Virginia

A large regional wholesale operation founded in the 1970s, selling gasoline under the Fleet-Wing brand name. Sohio purchased Spears & Riddle in 1928 and created the Fleet-Wing Corporation as a marketing subsidiary to brand jobbers in Ohio and surrounding states. Pennzoil purchased Fleet-Wing from Sohio about 1970 and continues to operate about a dozen stations under the Fleet-Wing name.

Fleet-Wing Ethyl (EGC) (15" Metal HP Blue)	1920-1928	$700-1,000
Fleet-wing That's All (Red 2pc Glass)	1928-1930	$2,000-2,600
Fleet-Wing Ethyl (red 2pc Glass)	1928-1930	$1,800-2,500
Say Fleet-Wing That's All (Red Hull)	1930-1933	$1,900-2,600
Fleet-Wing Ethyl (EGC) (Red Hull)	1930-1933	$1,800-2,400
Fleet-Wing (Red Ripple)	1933-1935	$1,600-2,100
Fleet-Wing Ethyl (EGC) (Red Ripple)	1933-1935	$1,600-2,100
Fleet-Wing (Red Hull)	1935-1938	$1,700-2,200
Fleet-Wing Ethyl (EGC) (Red Hull)	1935-1938	$1,600-2,100
Fleet-Wing Golden (13.5" Glass W)	1938-1946	$600-900
Fleet-Wing Super Ethyl (EGC) (13.5" Glass W)	1938-1946	$550-850
(Fleet-Wing) Flite (13.5" Glass W)	1938-1946	$500-800
(Fleet-Wing) Flite (13.5" Glass W)	1946-1955	$500-800
Fleet-Wing Golden (13.5" Glass W)	1946-1955	$500-800
Fleet-Wing Super (13.5" Glass W)	1946-1955	$500-800
Fleet-Wing (13.5" Glass W)	1955-1970	$350-600
Fleet-Wing (Red Capco)	1955-1970	$300-500
Fleet-Wing (Capco)	1955-1970	$250-450

Signs

Major Signs

Red Crown porcelain sign
30" Round,1926-1930. $400-600

Sohio sign, 1928-1934. Sign only, 4' x 2'. Panels, 6' x 1' each. Total, 15 ft. long. $1,500-2,000

Sohio Dealer sign, double-sided porcelain. 4 3/4' x 3', 1934-1945. $800-1,500

Sohio ID sign, 2' x 5', 1934-1945. $600-1,200

Sohio station sign. Double-sided porcelain, 1945-1962. $1,500-2,000

Sohio driveway sign. Single-sided porcelain, 7' x 5'. Holes for neon tubing. 1945-1962. $500-800

Sohio driveway sign. Double-sided, 6' x 4', 1962-1988. $250-375

Sohio station mounted sign. One-sided porcelain, 6' x 4', 1962-1988. $275-375

Sohio Road Sign. Single-sided tin, 5' x 5', 1962-1988. $250-350

Sohio driveway sign. Single-sided plastic, 6' x 4', 1962-1988. $250-350

Sohio/BP changeover logo. Plastic, 6' x 6', 1988-1990. This was the last Sohio ID to be taken down after re-branding. This logo appears to have been used for signage only. $250-350

Sohio Motor Oil Sign. Double-sided porcelain, 2' x 3 1/2', 1929-1939. $350-650

Standard Oil Penn roadside sign. Double-sided, 2 1/2' x 2', 1934-1946. $300-800

Above: Sohio High-test Ethyl. Double-sided porcelain, 2' x 3 1/2', 1928-1933. $350-650

Left: Sohio Ethyl Gasoline, Anti-Knock. Double-sided porcelain, 2' x 3 1/2', 1933-1936. $350-650

Sohio Ethyl Gasoline, Anti-Knock. Double-sided porcelain, 2' x 3 1/2', 1936-1940. $350-650

Sohio Motor Oil . Building mount sign, one-sided porcelain, 1928-1940. $250-450

General Use Signs

Sohio Boron ad sign. One-sided printed steel, 3 1/2' x 5', 1956-1962. $350-450

Standard oil dealer building sign. 5' x 1', 1928-1945. $375-475

Sohio roadside sign. Single-sided tin, 10' x 4', 1945-1962. $250-350

Oil Rack Signs

Sohio Motor Oil rack sign. 20 1/2" x 10", 1930-1946. $175-375

Standard Oil Penn Motor Oil rack sign. Double-sided, 20 1/2" x 10", 1933-1946. $150-350

Sohio HQD Oil rack sign. Double-sided, 15 1/2" x 10", 1952-1955. $100-200

Sohio Premex Oil rack sign. Double-sided, 15 1/2" x 10", 1955-1962. $150-250

Sohio Golden Duron Oil rack sign. Single-sided, 17 1/2" x 10 1/2", 1965-1968. $75-125

Sohio Duron Oil rack sign. Double-sided, 15 1/2" x 10", 1962-1964. $100-175

Sohio QVO Oil rack sign. One-sided, 17 1/2" x 10-1/2", 1968-1976. $75-150

Other Signs

Sohio oil well sign. One-sided porcelain, 1960. $125-225

Sohio Herd Oil sign. Tin, 2' x 1', 1953-1962. $75-125

Sohio oil well signs. Single-sided porcelain, 2' x 1'. $125-225

Atlas Brake Service. Single-sided, painted tin, 2' x 1 1/4', 1962-1986. $75-125

Operated by Sohio. Double-sided painted steel, 3' x 2 3/4', 1972-1988. Intended to show an outlet was company-owned and not a dealer. $125-325

Sohio ID sign. Masonite, 2 1/4' x 1 3/4', 1962-1988. $50-75

Super Boron pole sign. One-sided cardboard, 7 1/2' x 3', 1956-1961. $150-200

Sohio Horizon credit card ad pump topper, 1988. $25-35

Battigs Sohio Service sign. Painted on wood, 6 1/2' x 1', 1949. $125-150

Taxi Posters

These were used on the back of taxi cabs in the 1930s through the 1950s.

Sohio Motor Oil taxi poster sign, 1941. $75-125

Sohio free air taxi poster sign, 1943. $75-125

Sohio Station. Cleveland, Ohio, 1955.
Courtesy of Mr. Bruce Young.

Sohio taxicab ad, 1951. $65-75

Sohio taxicab ad, 1944. $65-75

Station and Jobber Use Items

Sohio Lubri charts and notebooks, 1941-1992. $15-75 each

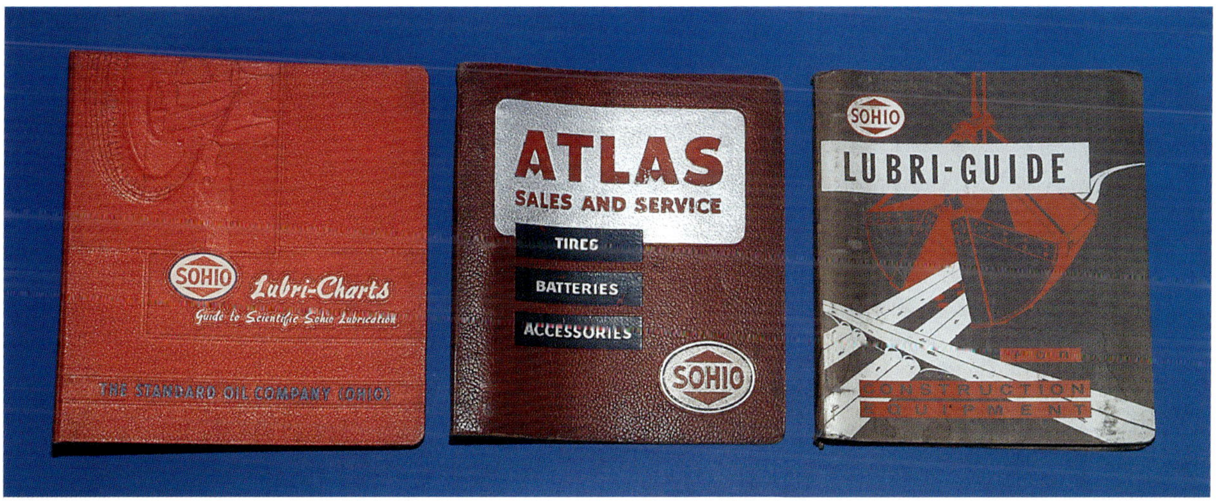

Sohio Island Store Experiment. This was an experimental venture of Sohio in July 1931 to sell products such as spark plugs, radiator chemicals, soap, light bulbs and other take-home items at the gas pump. No value established. *Courtesy Frank's Toy Box, Mentor, Ohio.*

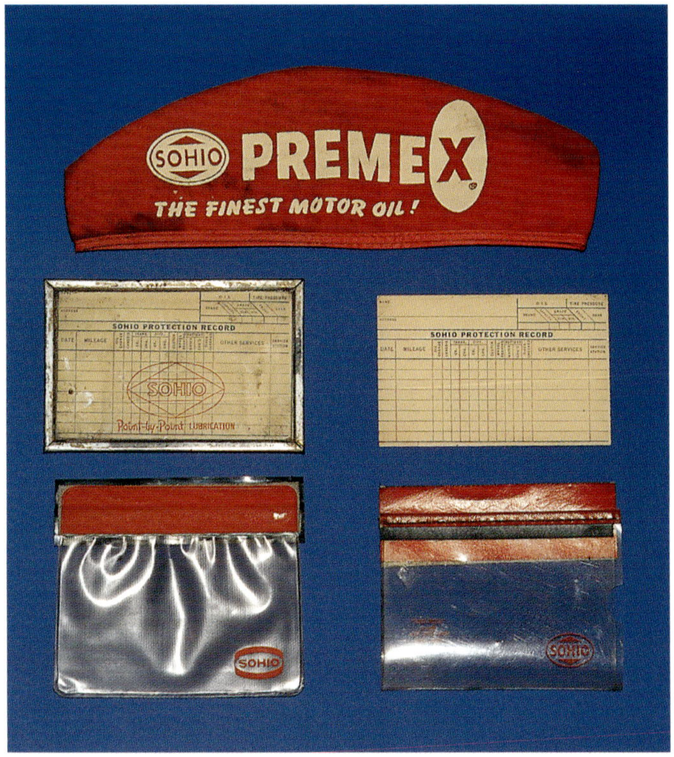

Top: Sohio Premex Hat, 1955, $35-45. Center row: Sohio private secretary record card and holder, 1948. $25-75. Bottom: Sohio under-hood record card holders, 1962 and 1959, $10-20 each.

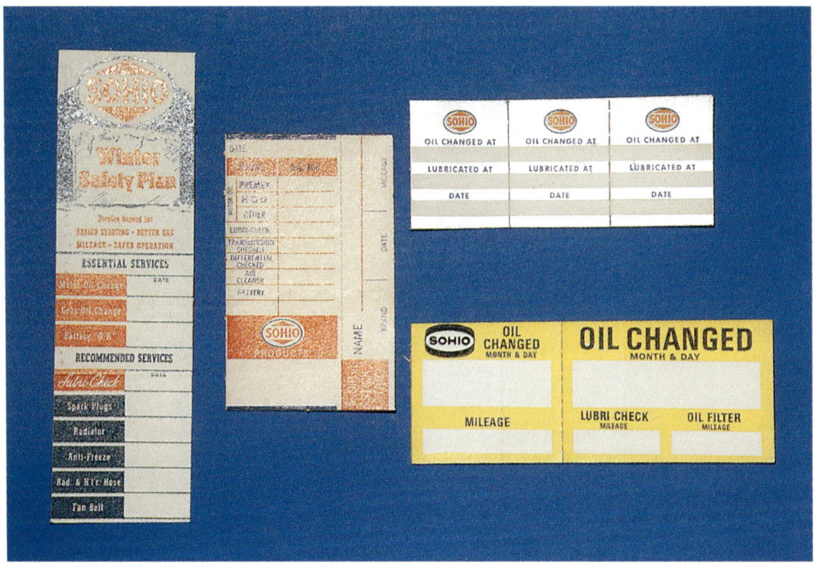

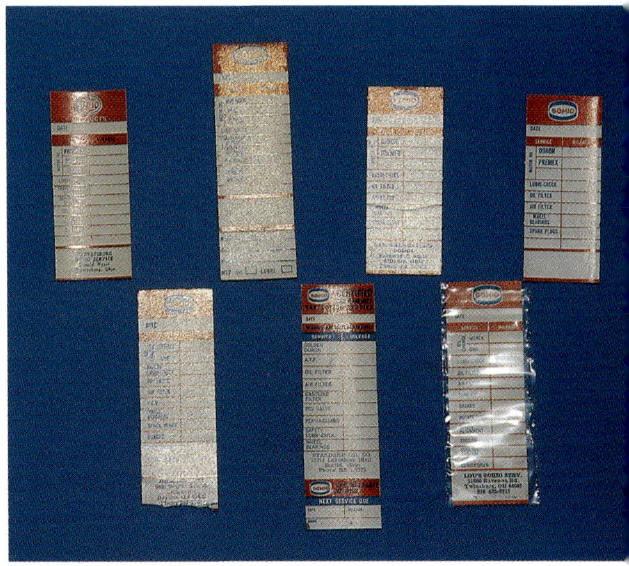

Sohio door jam stickers, 1943-1983, $5-15 each.

Box of Sohio door jam stickers, 1954. $25-45

Box of door jam stickers, 1965. $20-30

Sohio Progressive dealer magazines, 1951-1952. $10-25 each

Sohio Service Digest magazines, 1951-1952. $10-25 each.

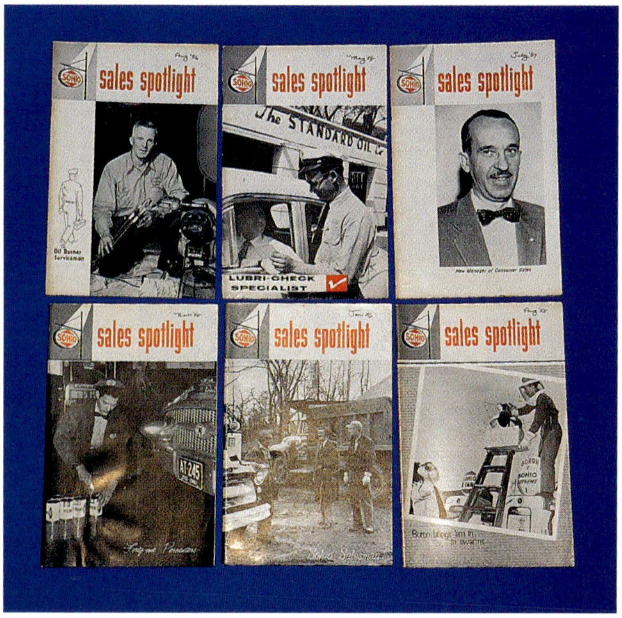

Various Sohio jobber and dealer publications, 1936-1962. $15-25 each.

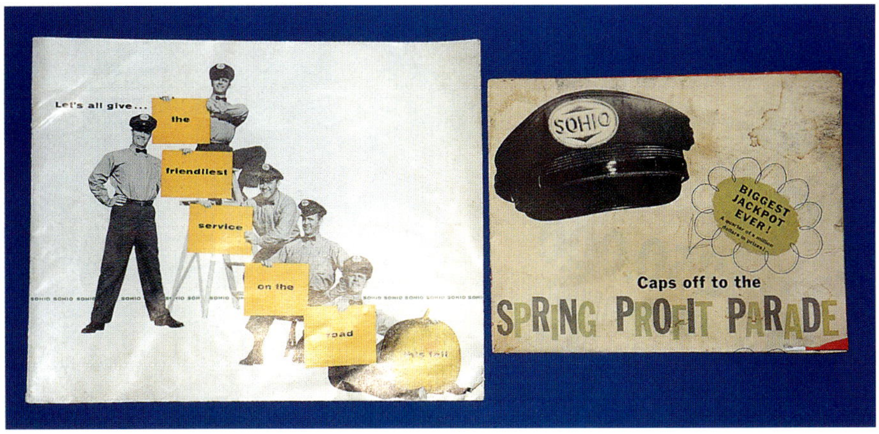

Sohio Spring Sales Plan, 1958. $20-30 both

Page from Sohio dealer book showing aftermarket products, 1951. $10-15

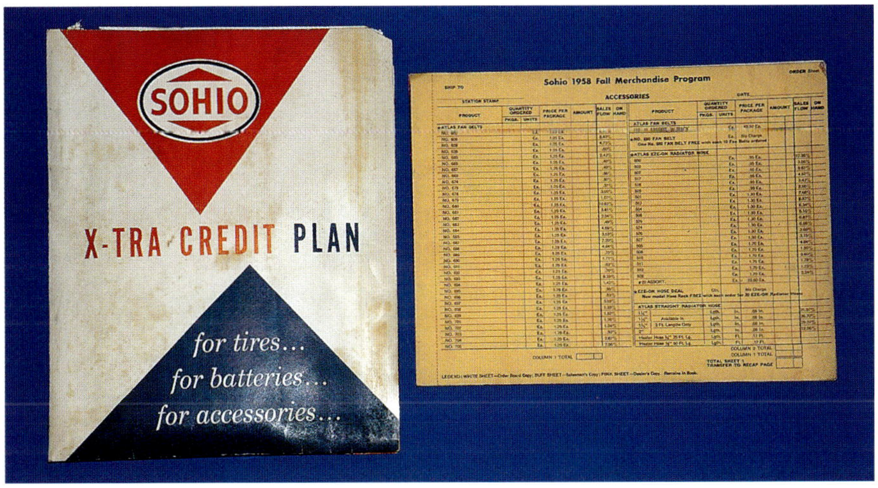

Left: Sohio X-tra Credit Plan forms and instructions with folder, 1958, $15-25.
Right: Sohio Fall 1958 Merchandise Program, order blank/inventory sheet, $10-20.

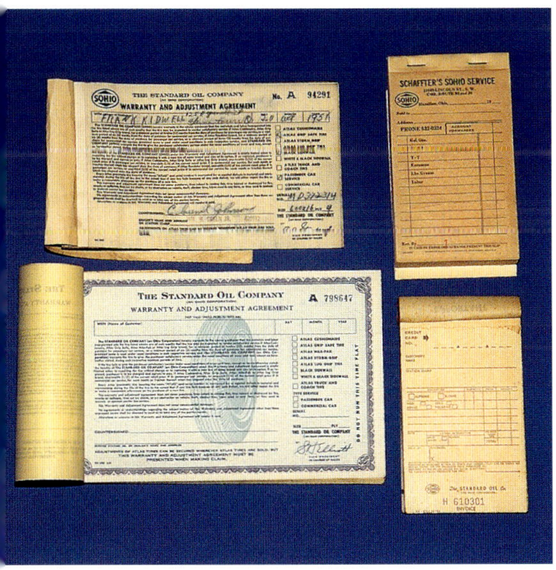

Sohio dealer forms, 1956. $10-20 each

Sohio dealer books, 1958. $25-35 each

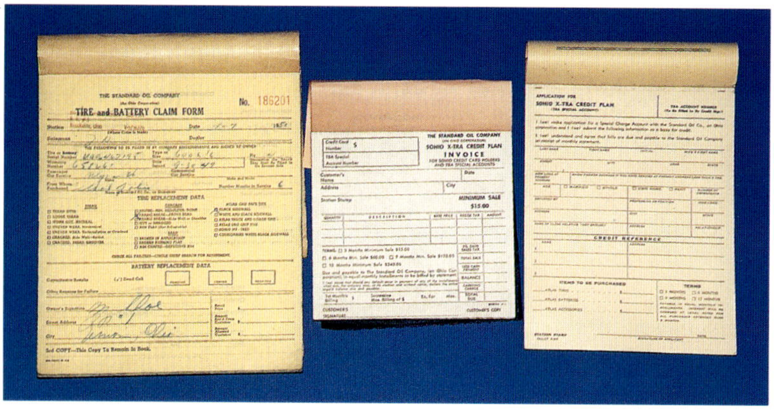

Sohio dealer forms, 1956. $10-20 each

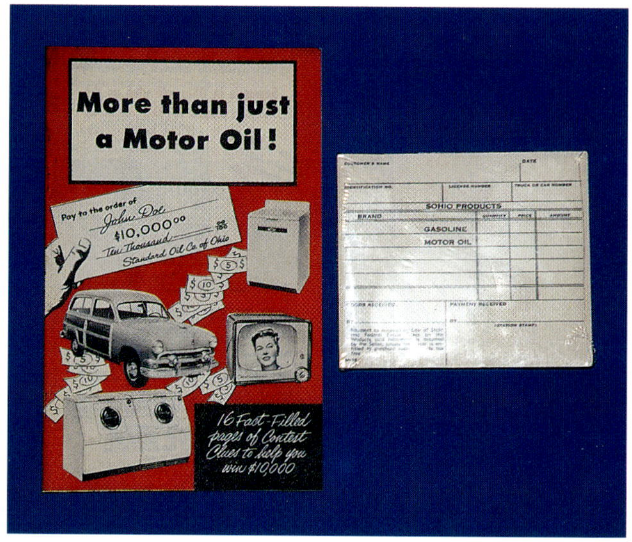

Sohio HQD info book and sales receipt pad, 1951 and 1961. $15-25

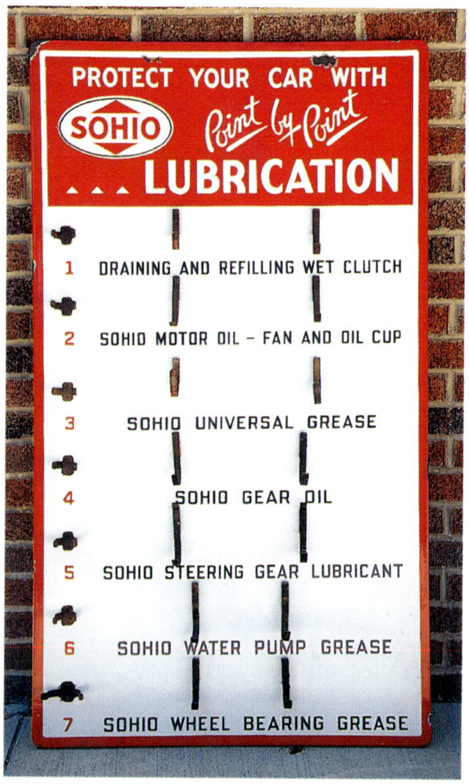

Sohio porcelain grease gun rack, 1940s, 2 3/4 x 4 1/2. $600-1,200 (with guns)

Sohio porcelain grease gun rack, 2 3/4 x 4 1/2, 1929-1939. $800-1,200

Left: Sohio Farm Oil Deal folder, 1952, $25-35. Center: Sohio Distributor Clipboard, 1950s, $15-25. Right: Sohio Farm Deal Oil order book, 1952, $25-35.

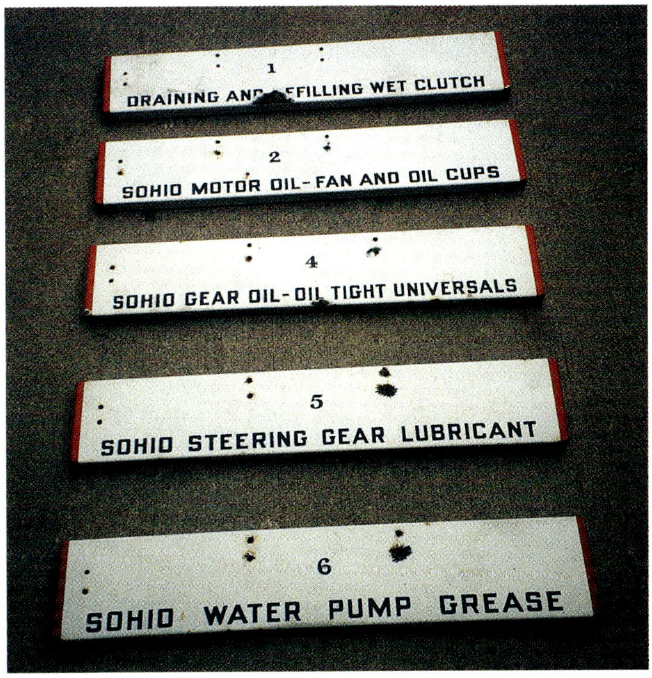

Wall mount porcelain grease gun holder set (#3 is missing), 1941. $350-550 set, $75-100 each.

Sohio double duty can, 5-gallon, 1953. $20-30

Sohio chassis lubricant, 100 lb. keg, 1949. $50-75

Sohio lube gear lube drum, 120 lbs., 1961. $25-35

Standard Oil of Ohio bulk oil can, 5-gallon, 1911-1928. $35-60

Left: Sohio double duty can, 5-gallon, 1959, $20-30.
Right: Sohio double duty can, 5-gallon, 1962, $25-35.

Sohio windshield service island cabinet, 1941. $150-250

Sohio windshield service cabinet, 1958. $175-275

So-Clear spray bottles, 8 oz., 1941. Left: No sprayer, $25-35. Right: With sprayer, $45-75.

So-Clear glass cleaner, 8-oz. bottle, 1957, $20-30. Right: So-Clear glass cleaner with sprayer, 8-oz. bottle, 1959, $35-45.

So-Clear glass cleaner, gallon-size. Left: 1955, $25-35. Right: 1958, $25-35

So-Clear windshield cabinet (plastic), 1969. $35-55

Tubeless tire solvent, 16-oz. can, 1953. $25-45

Sohio Westpet grease, 1-lb. can, 1946. $20-30

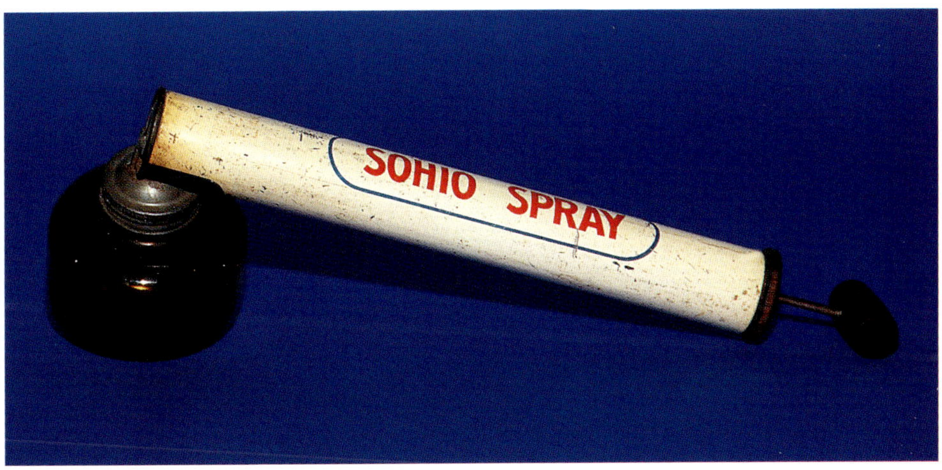

Sohio Spray hand sprayer, 1940. $25-45

Sohio station or lab sample test bottles, 1945/1955. $25-35 each

Sohio seat cover box, 1958. $25-30

Sohio gift box for auto or home accessories, 1953. $25-35

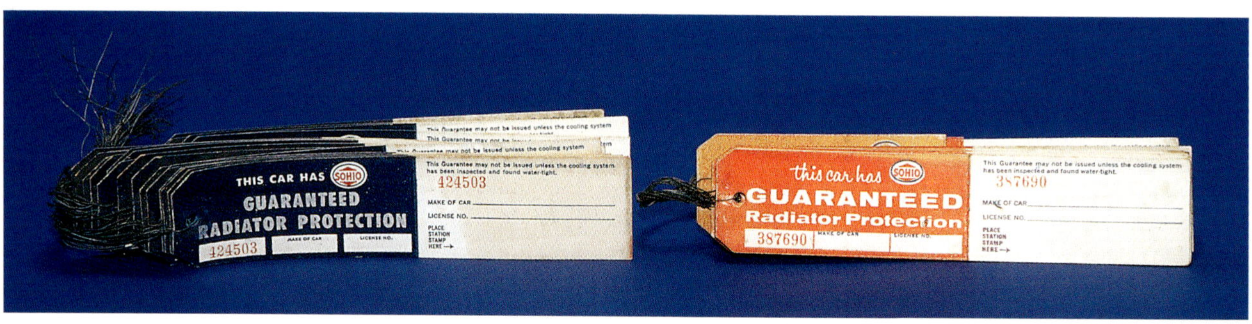

Sohio GRP radiator tags, 1953 and 1954. $5-10 each

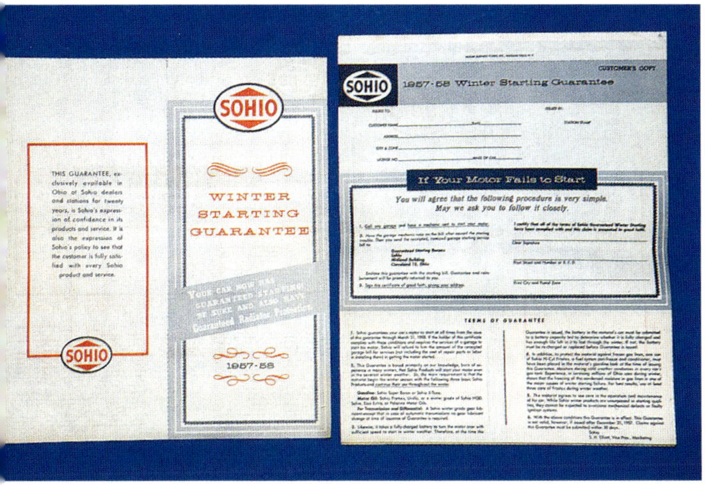

Sohio Guaranteed Starting certificates, 1955-1956 and 1957-1958. $10-15 each

Sohio Guaranteed Starting window poster, 1961. $10-15

Sohio Guaranteed Radiator Protection items, 1960-1967. $5-15 each

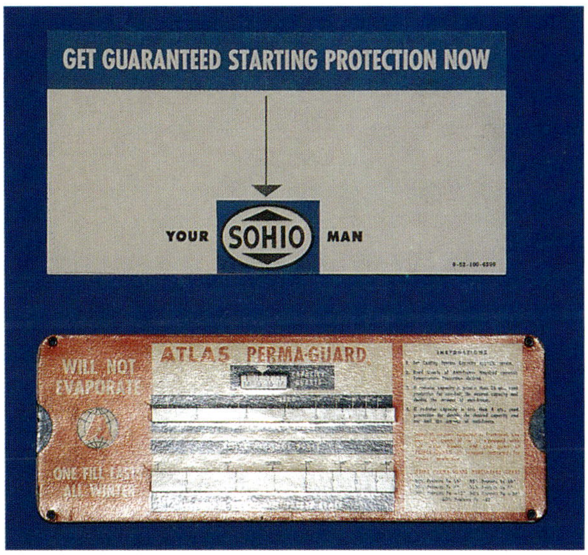

Atlas Perma-Guard slide rule and Guaranteed Starting flyer, 1960. $5-15 each

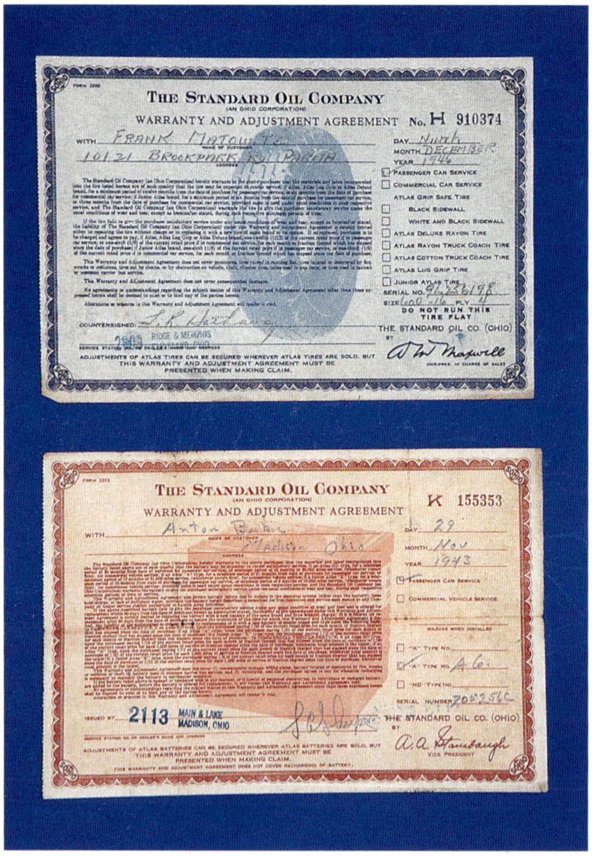

Sohio tire and battery warranties, 1948-1968. $5-10 each

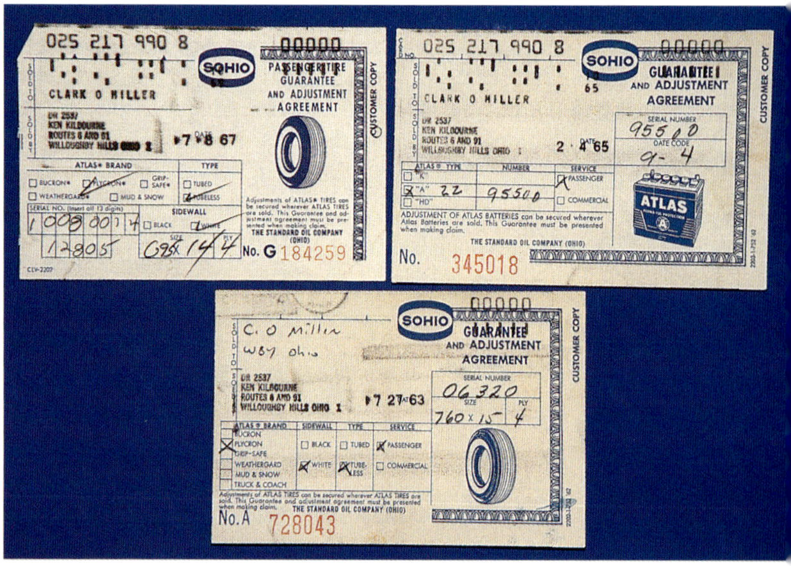

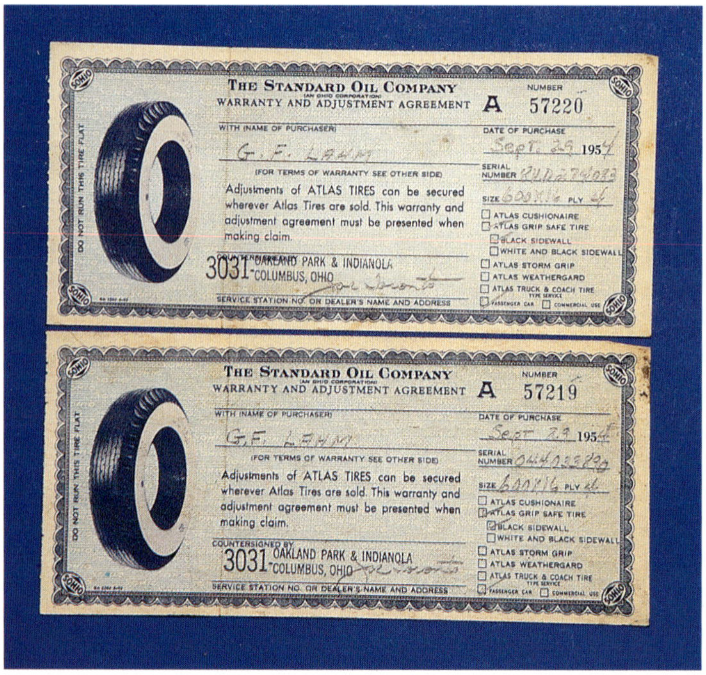

Sohio tire and battery warranty envelopes, 1953-1983. $5-10 each

Sohio tire adjustment guide and sales folder, 1965. $5-15 each

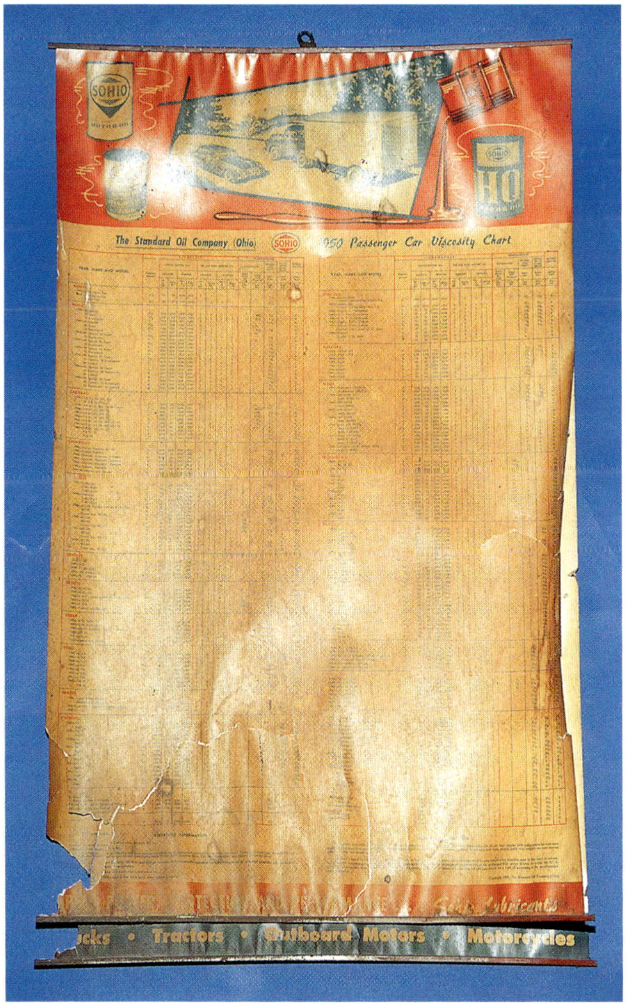

Sohio HQ capacities wall chart, 1950. $15-30

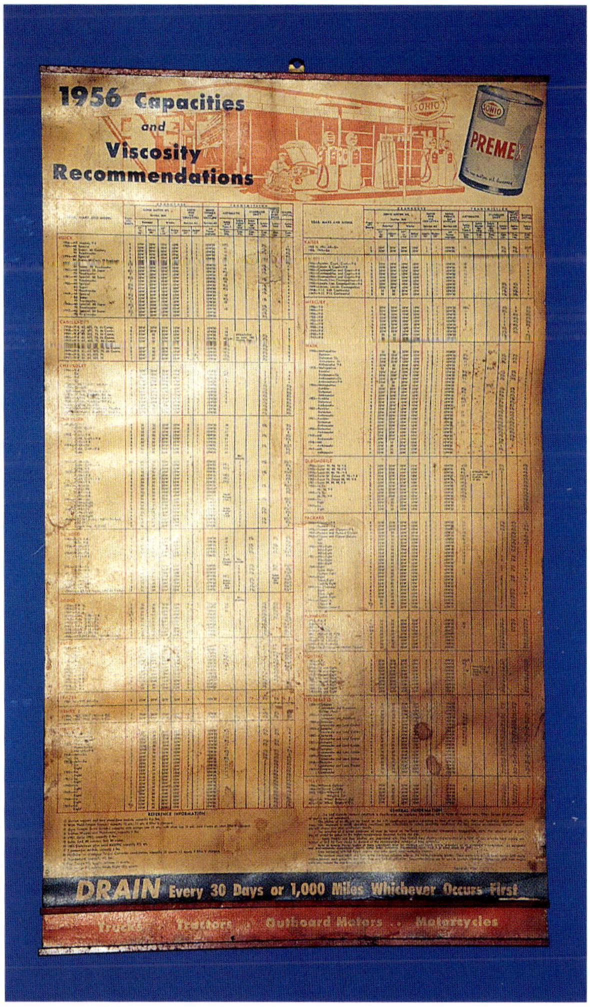

Sohio Premex capacities wall chart, 1956. $15-30

Above and Below: Sohio envelopes, 1954-1984. $5-10 each

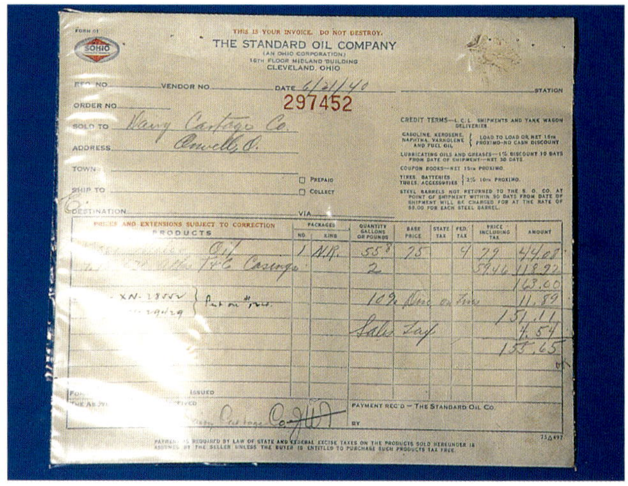

Sohio service invoice, 1941. $5-10

Boron pump topper (fits over pump globe), 1961. #35-65

Boron with Ice Gard pump topper, 1961. $35-65

Sohio Guaranteed Starting banner, 1946. $75-125

Sohio "All Out Spring Special" banner, 1953. $75-125

"You Start or We Pay" banner, 1949. $75-125

Sohio Premex cardboard sign, 1956. $50-75

Sohio Xtane and Supreme banner, 1951. $75-125.

"Boron Cleans Your Carburetor" banner, 1961. $75-100

Contest Items

Sohio Double License Plate Jackpot winners list dealer kit, March 1967. $25-30

Assortment of Sohio/Boron game pieces, 1967-1969. $5-8 each

Sohio License Plate Jackpot winners station poster, 1967. $5-10

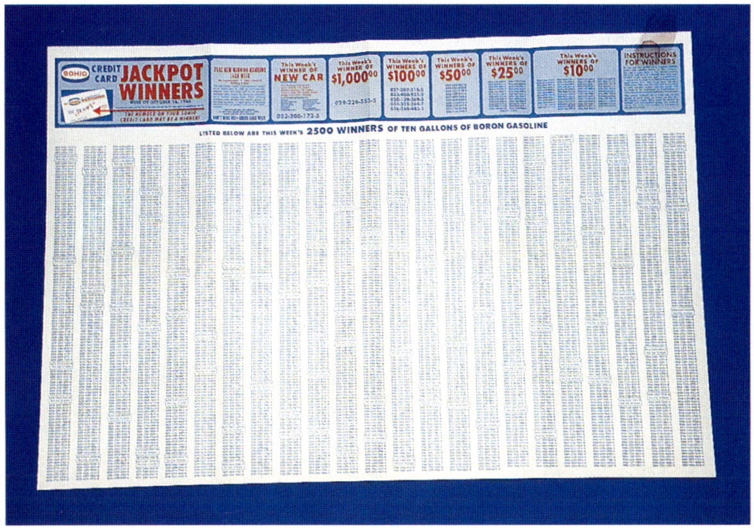

Above and Right: Sohio Credit Card Jackpot winners list and dealer kit, October 1966. $25-30

Boron Oil Division Credit Card Jackpot station ads, 1967. $5-10 each

---

Dealer Supplies

Sohio drum hole covers, 1960. $5-10 each

Sohio lock and Sohio motor oil drum cap, 1929. $50-75 each.

Sohio Super Filter gas filter, 1966. $25-45

Sohio dipstick napkin, 1950s. $5-10

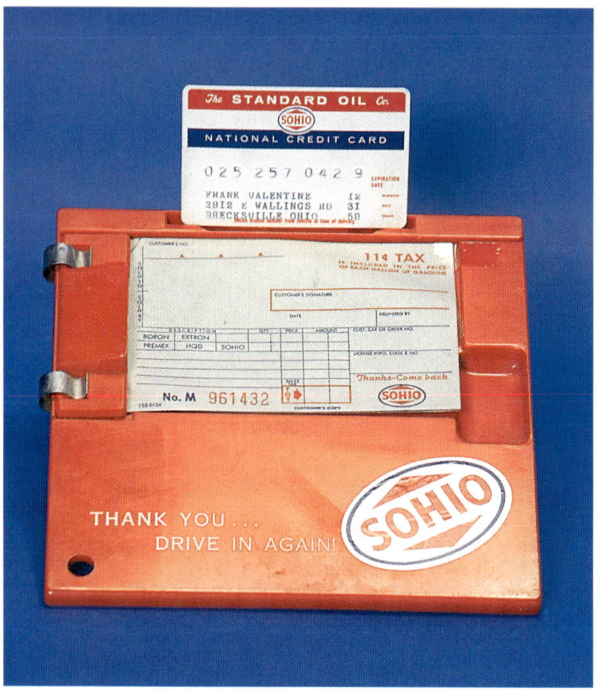

Sohio credit card clipboard with credit card, 1961. $45-65

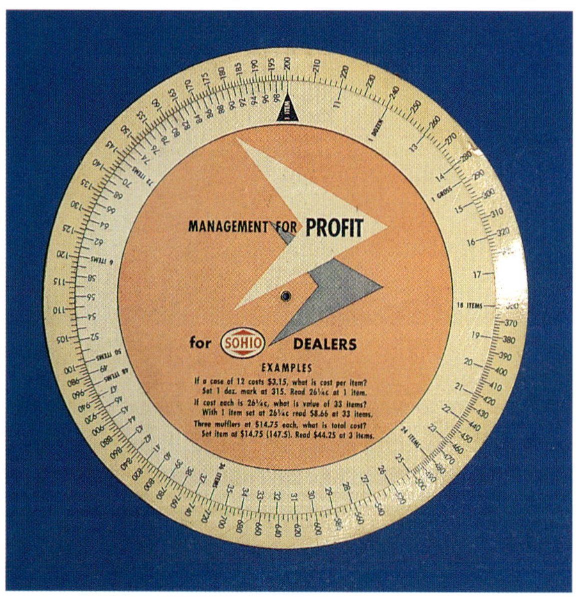

Sohio products gallonage calculator, 1955. $15-25

Sohio G.S. Man pinback, given to station attendants for providing good service to customers, 1938. $75-125

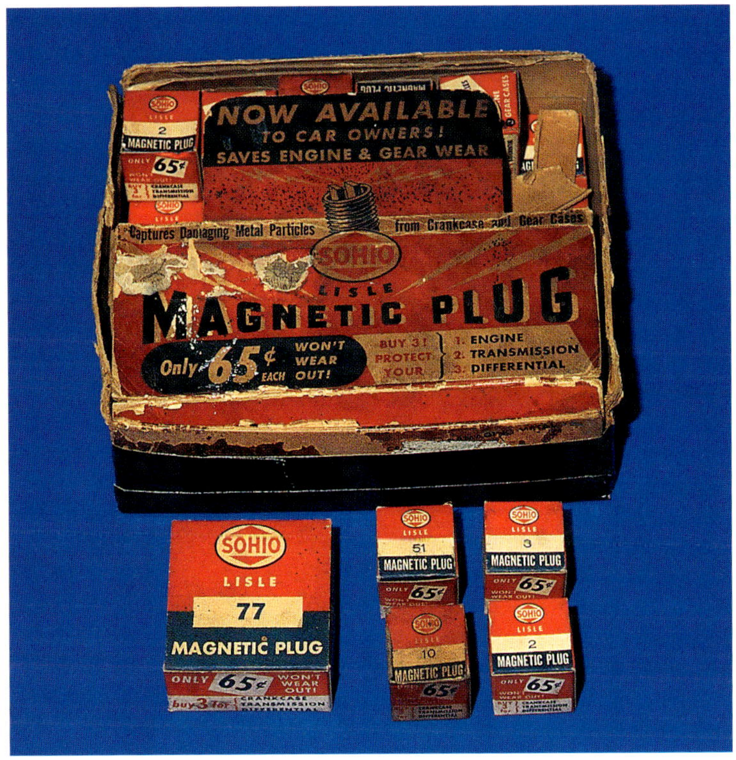

Sohio magnetic plugs, 1946. Used to trap metal deposits from motors, transmissions, and gear boxes. Box with plugs, $125-175. Plugs, $5-10 each.

Sohio liquid soap, 1959. $50-75

Sohio dealer wall clock, 1949. $75-150

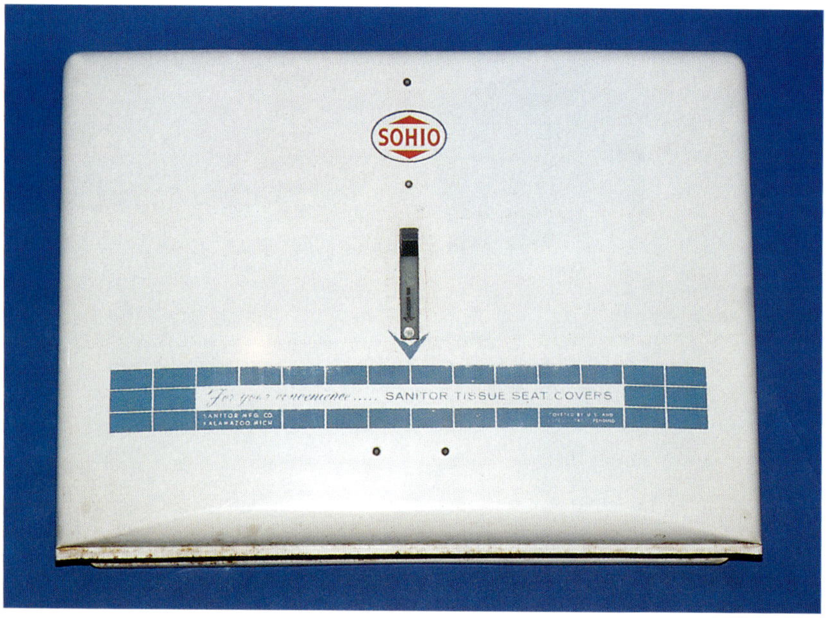

Sohio restroom toilet seat cover dispenser, 1960. $125-175

Employee & Station Awards

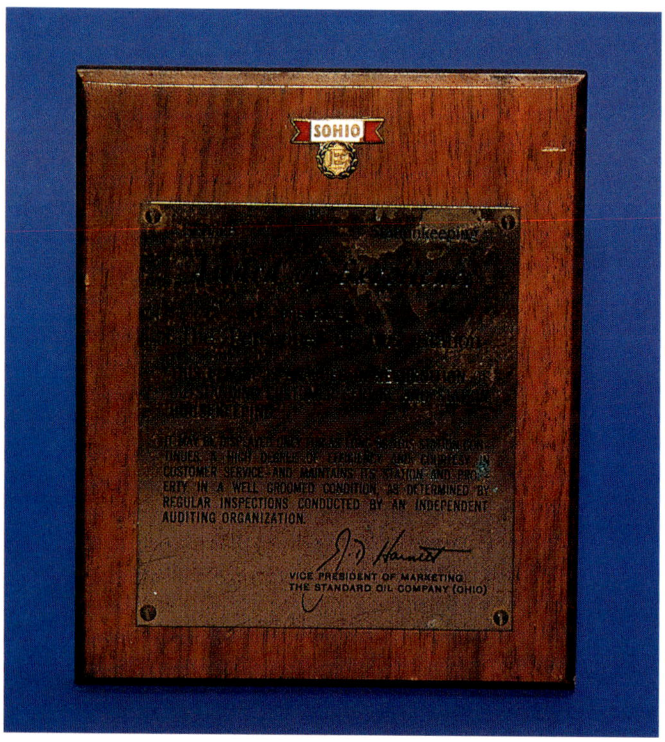

Sohio Excellence award, 1960s. $35-45

Sohio service award, 30 years, 1959. $25-45

Sohio service award, 10 years. $25-45

Sohio service awards, 1950-1960. $25-45 each

Sohio service pins, 1935-1985. $50-150 each

Uniforms

Sohio long wool coat, 1928-1945. $275-325

Sohio service station attendant's cap, 1957. $125-225

Sohio woman's summer hat, 1961. $35-45

Sohio winter attendant's cap, 1961. $50-75

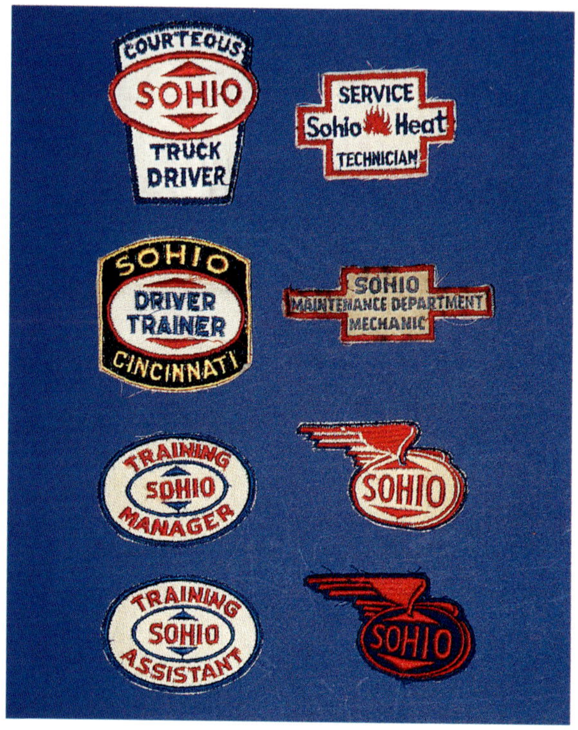

Sohio jacket patches, 1950-1962. $10-20 each

Sohio jacket patches, 1928-1962. $10-20 each

Sohio jacket patches, 1962-1980s. $5-10

Sohio shirts and jackets, 1955-1985. $50-125 each

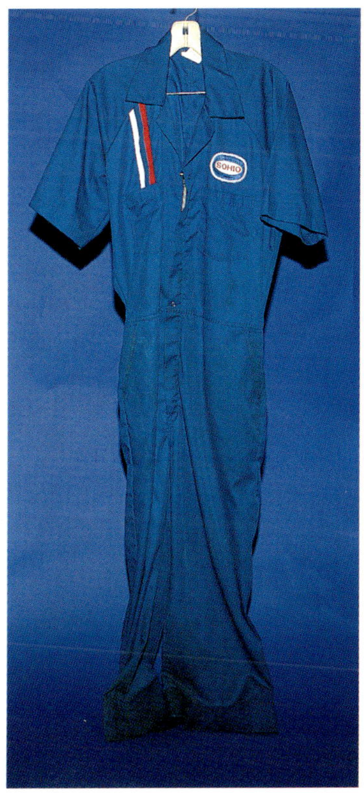

Employee Publications & Other Items

Various Employee Publications (*The Sohioan*), 1930s-1950s. $15-25 each. The *Sohioan* was a monthly company news magazine for employees and stockholders.

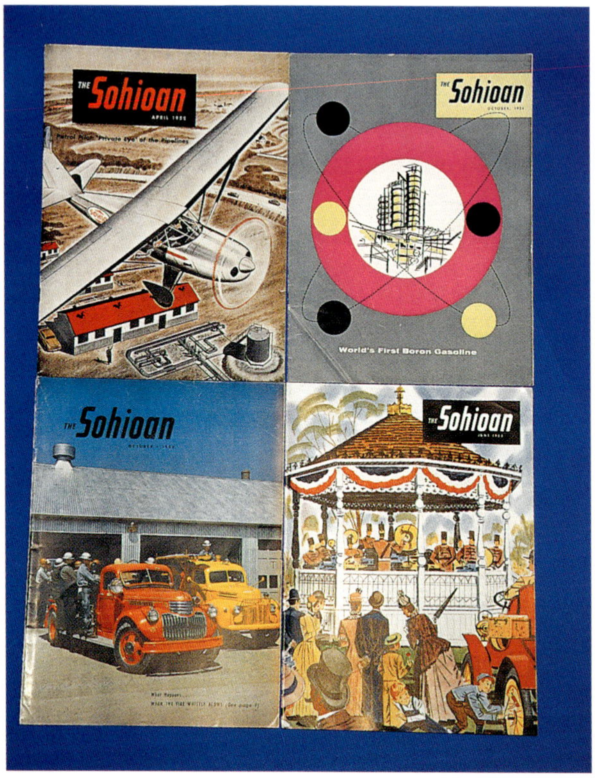

Left: *The Sohioan* 75th Anniversary issue, 1945, $25-35.
Right: *The Sohioan* Centennial issue, 1970, $25-30.

Left: Sohio visitors badge, 1960, $20-30.
Right: Sohio automatic transmission specialist badge, 1961, $25-50.

Sohio employee items, 1940, 1944, 1961. $25-50 each

Sohio cufflink and tie bar set, 1958. $125-150

Sohio Safety Week record, 1960. $10-20

Sohio golf balls, 1970. $10-20

Sohio Quarter Century Club

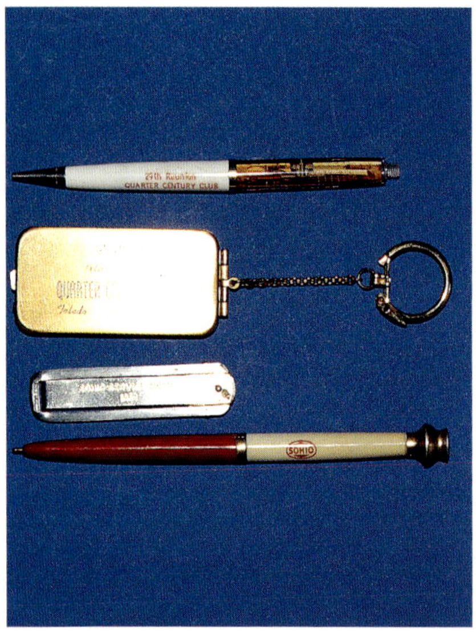

Sohio Quarter Century Club giveaways, 1950-1960. $20-35 each

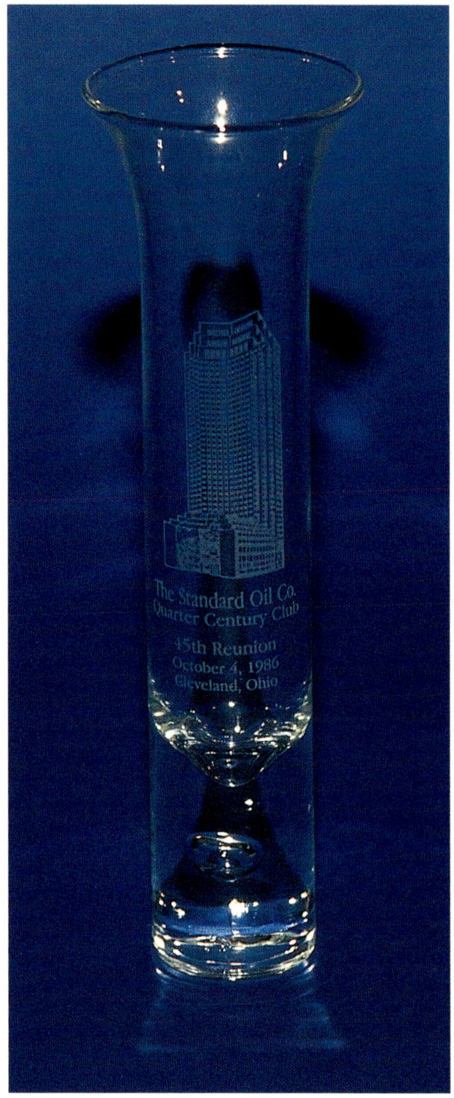

Quarter Century Club 45th Reunion bud vase, 1986. $15-25

Left: Quarter Century Club, Cincinnati division clock, 1988, $10-20. Right: Sohio Diesel Supreme Clock, 1978. $10-20

Sohio Outboard motor oil window poster, 1956. $75-100

Sohio HQ ad, 1943. $5-15

Boron Gasoline original artwork, 1959. $125-195

Boron Gasoline ad, original artwork, 1958. $125-175

Boron with Ice-gard, original artwork, 1961. $125-195

Sohio Farmex and S-3 HD ads, 1954. $10-15

Sohio HQD ad from *Ohio Farmer* magazine, 1957. $5-15

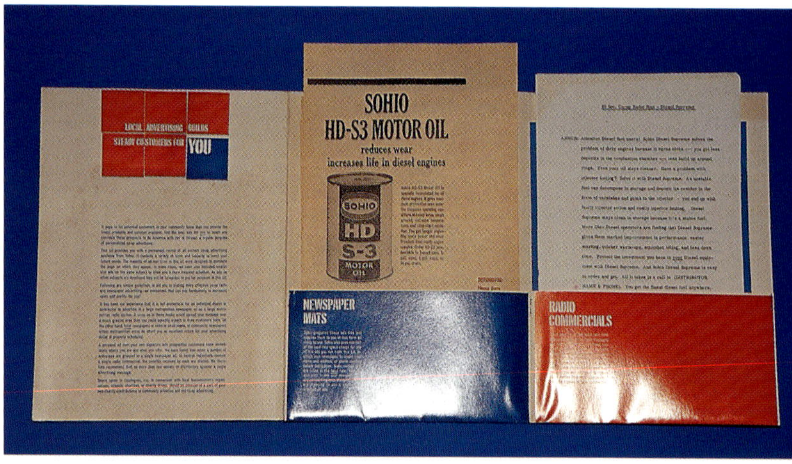

Sohio farm products ad kit, 1963. $35-45

Boron introductory ad, 1956. $10-15

Sohio post cards, 1945-1963. $5-35 each

Sohio mailer, sent to buyers of new 1941 Cadillacs, selling Sohio Supreme. $20-30

Left: Sohio printer's block, 1934-1945, $25-45.
Right: Sohio HQD printer's block, 1951, $25-50.

Miniature Signs

Sohio custom-made miniature neon sign. 1928-1945 logo by Chris McKee of Dearborn, Michigan. No established value.

Another Chris McKee creation. Custom-made neon light-up sign, 1945-1962 logo. No established value.

'New' Sohio Toys

Ertl 1931 Hawkeye Tanker #2879. 1250 produced. $50

Ertl 1938 Chevy Panel #3940. 800 produced. $75

JLE Scale Models 1931 IHC tanker, #6B4105. 1250 produced. $75

Ertl 1925 Kenworth barrel truck, #B762UO. 1250 produced. $45

First Gear 1957 IHC tanker, #19-1464. 1800 produced. $125

First Gear 1957 IHC wrecker, #19-1581. 1410 produced. $125

First Gear 1951 Ford aviation tanker, #19-1763. 1570 produced. $45

First Gear 1960 B-Model Mack semi tanker, #19-1916. 1260 produced. $100

First Gear 1953 White 3000 semi tractor trailer, #19-1908. 1260 produced. $60

First Gear 1959 IHC semi van tractor trailer, #18-1909. 1260 produced. $60

First Gear 1951 Ford fire truck (Lima), #18-1925. $60

Ertl 1940 Ford pipeline truck, #H619UO. 1250 produced. $50

First Gear 1953 White 3000 tanker, #29-2109. 1260 produced. $55

First Gear 1960 B Model wrecker, #19-2232. 900 produced. $75

First Gear 1960 B Model fire truck, #19-2253. 900 produced. $75

First Gear 1969-1973 R Model Mack tanker, #19-2367. 1260 produced. $60

Ertl DC-3 airplane #H020T0, 1250 produced, $50. Sohio airplane hanger by Vees Collectibles, 100 produced, $50.

Sohio gas station by Vees Collectibles. 150 produced. $50

Sohio Supreme and Sohio X70 gas pumps by Vees Collectibles. 1250 of each produced. $35 each

A special thank you to Lynn and Sandy Oakley at S-O toys for the information and prices of these wonderful toys.

1926 Mack Bulldog truck bank, Lima Refinery, by Ertl. Year of issue not known. $35-65

1930s Sohio plastic tank truck, by Marx. Has working head and tail lamps. $50-65

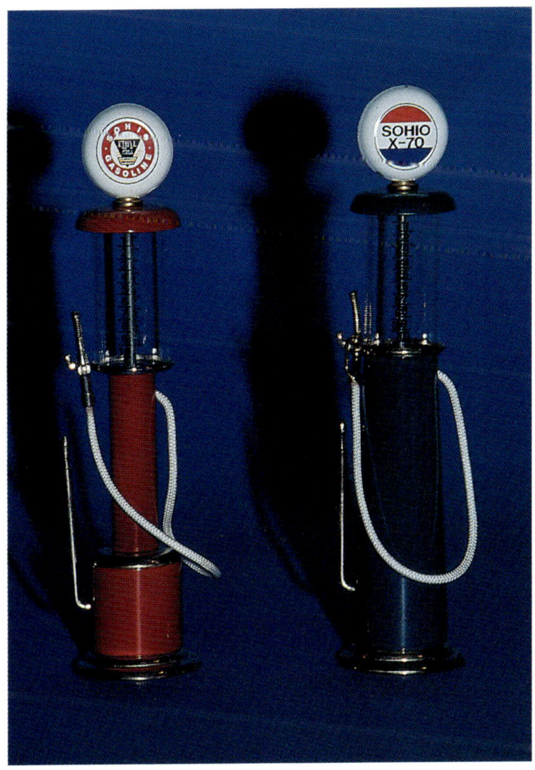

Sohio toy gas pumps. Manufacturer not known. $25-45 each

Chapter Six
Company Divisions

Fleetwing motor oil. 1-quart glass bottle, 1942-1945. $75-100

Fleet-Wing

Fleet-Wing was a jobber-secondary brand from 1928-1975.

Fleet-Wing Oil, 1-quart cans, 1949. $35-100 each

Fleet-Wing Piston Seal, 5-quart can, 1952. $35-75

Fleet-Wing "New" Certified, 1-quart can, 1951. $25-45

Fleet-Wing Oil, 1-quart cans, 1963. $25-35 each

Fleet-Wing Oil, 1-quart cans, 1970. $25-35 each

Fleet-Wing, 2-gallon cans, 1940-1960.
$25-45 each

Fleet-Wing Super Antifreeze, 1-quart can, 1941. $75-125

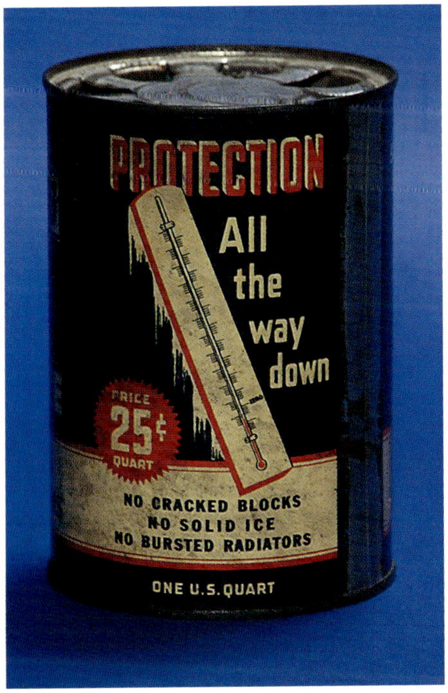

Fleet-Wing Super Antifreeze, side view, 1-quart can, 1941. $75-125

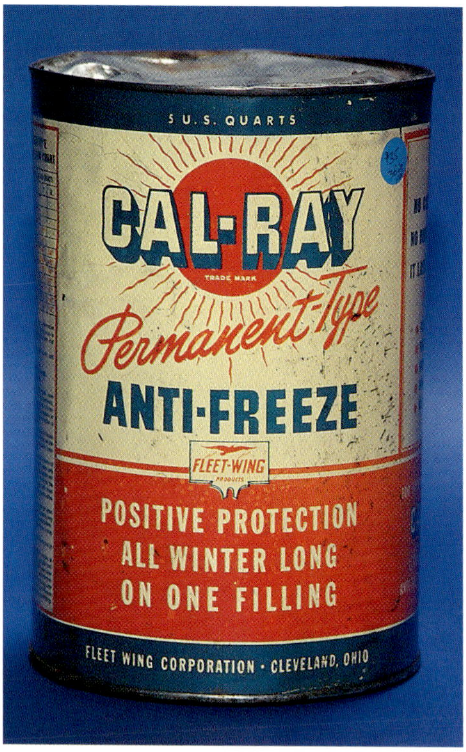

Fleet-Wing Cal-Ray Antifreeze, 1951. $45-75

Fleet-Wing Pressure Gun Grease, 5-lb. can, 1949. $30-50

Fleet-Wing Grease, 5-lb. can, 1955. $20-40

Left: Fleet-Wing Masterlube, 1-lb. can, 1955, $25-55.
Right: Fleet-Wing Grease, 1-lb. can, 1955. $25-35

Fleet-Wing Masterlube, 1-lb. cans, 1961-1965. $20-30 each

Fleet-Wing Auto Polish, 1-pint bottle, 1942-1945. $20-30

Fleet-Wing Top Cylinder Lubricant, 1-pint bottle, 1950. $35-65

Fleet-Wing Utility Oil, 4-oz. can, 1959. $50-100

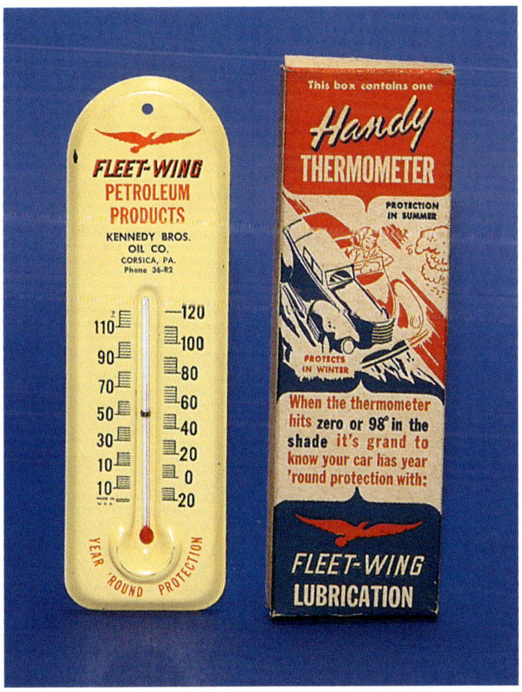

Fleet-Wing Thermometer, 10", 1957. $50-75

Fleet-Wing maps, stickers, blotters, matches, cards, 1941-1971. $3-25 each

Fleet-Wing customized license plate, 1961. $25-35

Fleet-Wing Lube Guide and Operator's Product Manual, 1971. $15-25 each

Fleet-Wing Super MG. Double-sided, painted tin, 1 3/4' x 2 1/2', 1962. $175-275

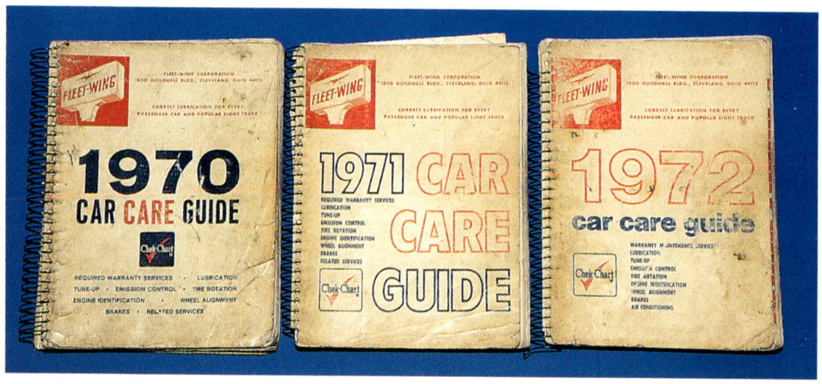

Fleet-Wing Car Care Guides. 1970, 1971, 1972. $10-20 each

Fleet-Wing Motor Oil sign. Pressed tin, 4' x 3', 1947. $125-225

Fleet-Wing MG. Double-sided, painted tin, 1 3/4' x 2 1/2', 1962. $175-275

Fleet-Wing 8-10 pump sign, 1954. $65-125

Fleet-Wing Driveway Sign. Double-sided plastic, 7' x 4', 1962. $250-350

Boron

These are some of the few of the Boron cans known to exist as in 1964. Sohio designed the generic cans so they could be used at both Boron and Sohio stations.

Boron Motor Oil, 1-quart cans, 1975. $5-10 each

Climaguard Motor Oil, Climaguard Oil Division—BP Oil Co., 1975. $10-20

Wm. Penn

A 1930s gas station of an unknown location. Wm. Penn was a Canfield Oil Company brand name. Standard Oil purchased Canfield Oil, a Cleveland-based company, in 1955, and the name was re-branded.

Wm. Penn oil cans, 1 quart, 1970. $20-35 each

Wm. Penn oil cans, 1-quart, 1955-1965. $25-35

Wm. Penn oil cans, 1 quart, 1975. $15-25 each

Left: Wm. Penn #3 Cup Grease, 1-lb. can, 1955, $20-40. Right: Wm. Penn grease, 5-lb. can, 1959, $20-30.

Wm. Penn Valve Ease, 1-pint cans. Left: 1952-1959, $20-30. Right: 1960, $20-30.

Left and center: Wm. Penn Frostex, 1961/1963, $10-20 each. Right: Wm. Penn Radiator Solder, 1963, $10-20.

Left: Wm. Penn Home Oiler, 4-oz. can, 1963, $25-35. Right: Wm. Penn Lighter Fluid, 4-oz. can, 1963, $25-35.

Left: Wm. Penn Outboard Motor Oil, plastic bottle, 1962, $10-15. Right: Wm. Penn Ice Remover Spray, 1965, $10-15.

Canfield

Sohio purchased Canfield in 1945 and by 1955 all Canfield stations were re-branded Sohio.

Canfield Dependable Penn, 2 variations, 1-quart can, 1950. $25-50 each

Canfield oil cans, 1-quart, 1940-1950. $25-50 each

Canfield Premium. Left: 1-quart can, 1950, $35-45. Right: Canfield Premium, 1/2-quart can, 1950, $25-30.

Canfield Premium, for sports and racing cars. 1/2-quart can, 1950. $25-45

Assortment of Canfield 1-quart cans, 1963. $20-30

Canfield Cleaning Fluid, 1-gallon can, 1939. $25-45

Left: Canfield Household Hints, 1936, $10-15. Right: Canfield road map, 1938, $10-15.

BP cans. These are the only BP quart cans known to be marketed in Ohio as they used plastic bottles in 1989. Vanellus US HD oils, 1-quart cans, 1986. $5-15 each

Other Sohio Divisions

These railroad cars representing the other Sohio divisions and operations are one-of-a-kind. The train set was custom-built by a former employee of the Sohio Transportation Department in 1976 and it was on display in Sohio's corporate headquarters for many years. It was purchased in 1999 and is a proud part of the collection. No value can be established for this set.

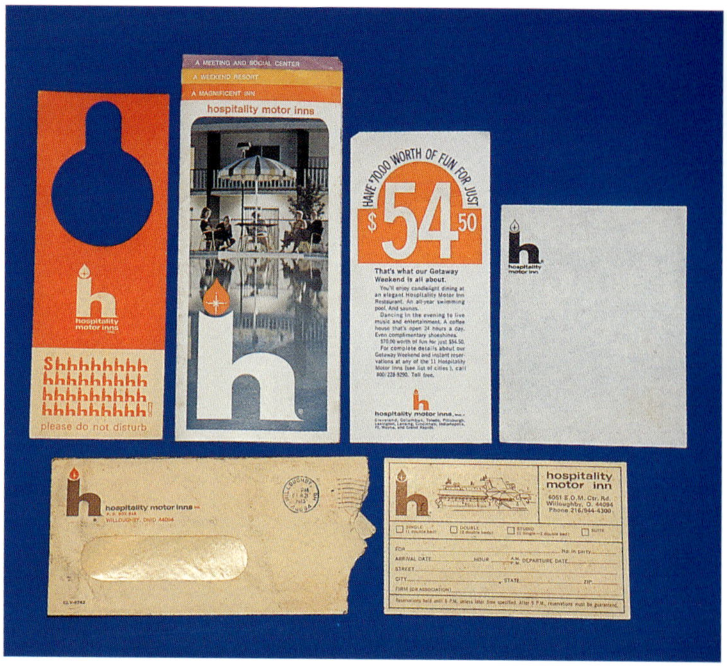

Hospitality Motor Inns were built by Sohio in 1965 and later sold to Harley Hotels.

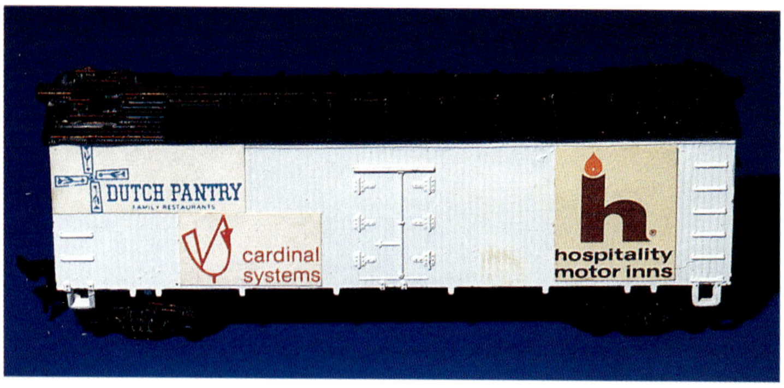

Box car. Dutch Pantry, Hospitality Motor Inns, Cardinal Systems (food service).

Parah Shale Co. Car.

Alyeska transport car (Alaska pipeline).

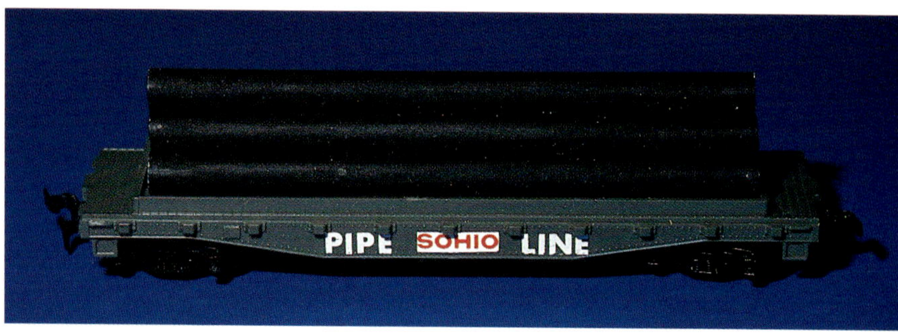

Sohio Pipeline Co. pipe car.

Old Ben Coal Co. coal car.

Reserve Mining ore car.

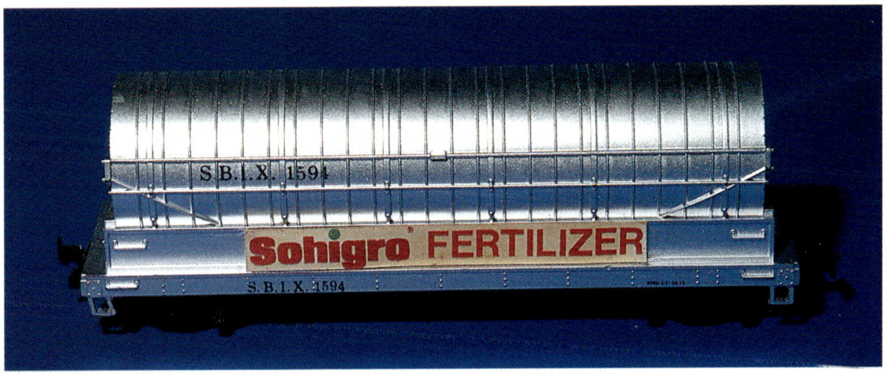

Sohigro fertilizer container car.

Plastics division, Vistron Barex 210 bottle resin trailers (for export).

Plastics division, Vistron Filon Silmar box car.

Plastics division, Vistron Pro Guard box car (brushes).

Shirt/jacket patch from MOCAR, Uranium Mining Division.

Atlas

The Atlas Supply Co. was established in the late 1920s as a co-op to supply all of the Standard Oil divisions with TBA items.

Atlas Perma-Guard Antifreeze, 1-gallon cans. Left: 1952, $15-25. Right: 1954, $15-25.

Atlas Perma-Guard Antifreeze, 1-gallon can, 1939. $15-25

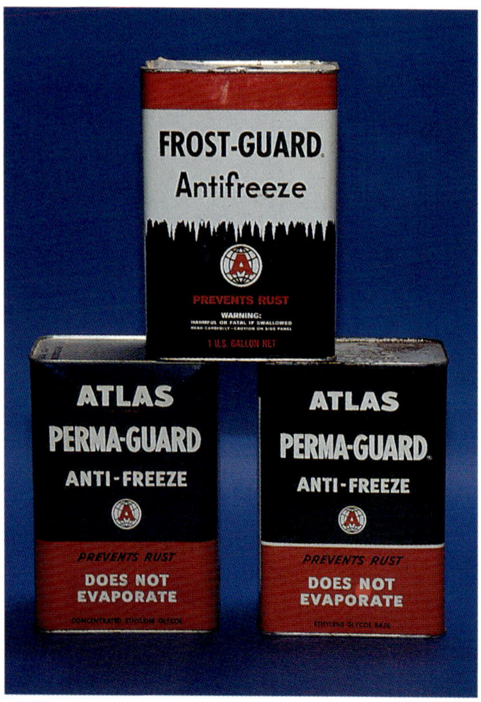

Atlas Antifreeze, 1-gallon cans. Top: Frost-Guard, 1950s, $15-25. Bottom left: Perma-Guard, 1956, $25-30. Bottom right: Perma-Guard, 1957, $15-25.

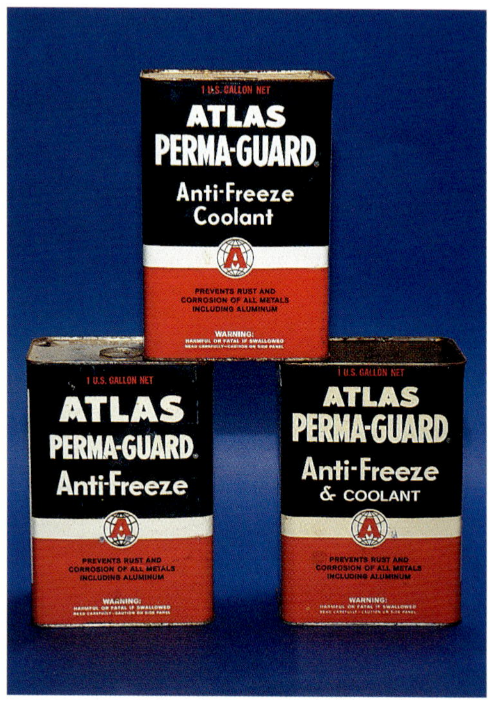

Atlas Perma-Guard Antifreeze (bottom left), 1-gallon can, 1963, $15-25. Atlas Perma-Guard Antifreeze & Coolant, 1-gallon cans, 1966 (bottom right) and 1968 (top), $15-25.

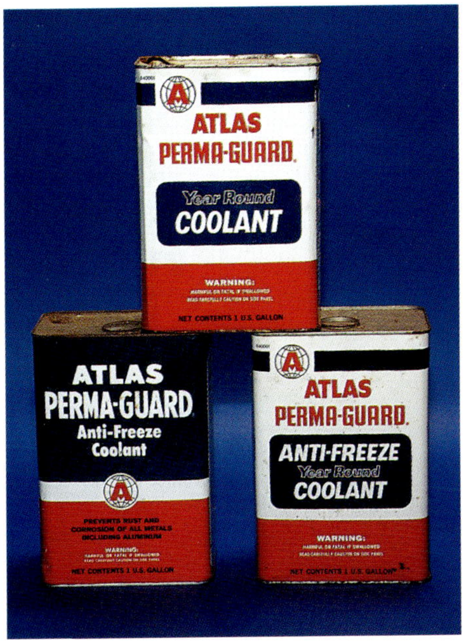

Atlas Perma-Guard Antifreeze and Coolant. Bottom left: 1969. Top and bottom right: 1971 (front and back views). $15-25 each

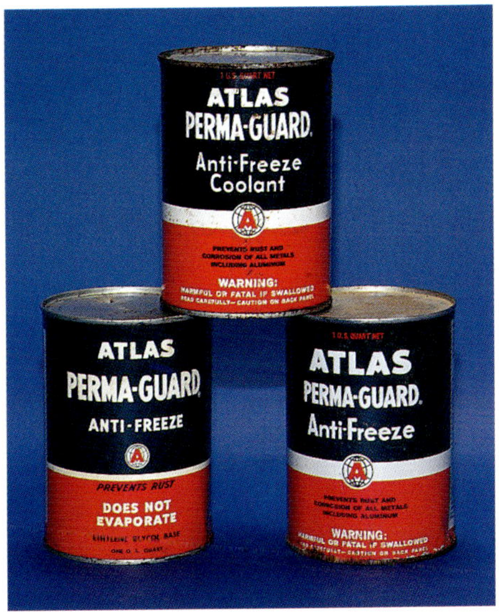

Atlas Perma-Guard Antifreeze, 1-quart cans, 1968, 1957, 1966. $15-30 each

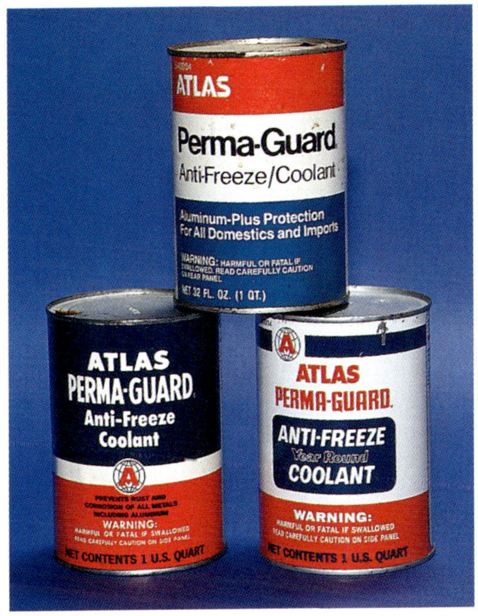

Atlas Permaguard Antifreeze, 1-quart cans, 1975, 1969, 1971. $15-25 each

Atlas Cooling System Cleaners, 16-oz. cans, 1962-1969. $10-15 each

Atlas Cooling System Solder, 12-oz. cans, 1962-1969. $10-15 each

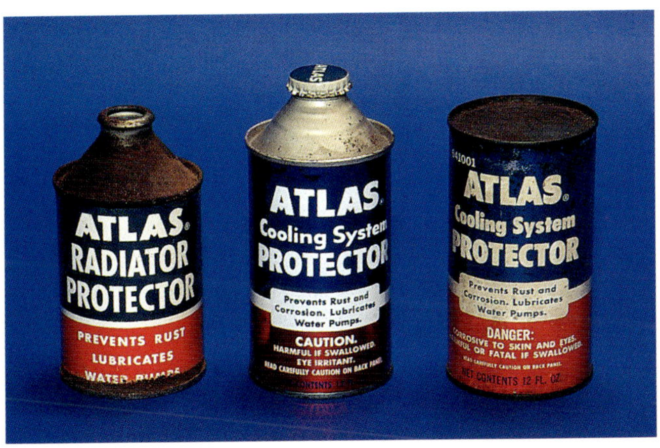

Atlas Cooling System Protector, 12-oz. cans, 1950s-1960s. $10-15 each

Atlas Block Sealer, 16-oz. cans, 1962-1969. $10-15 each

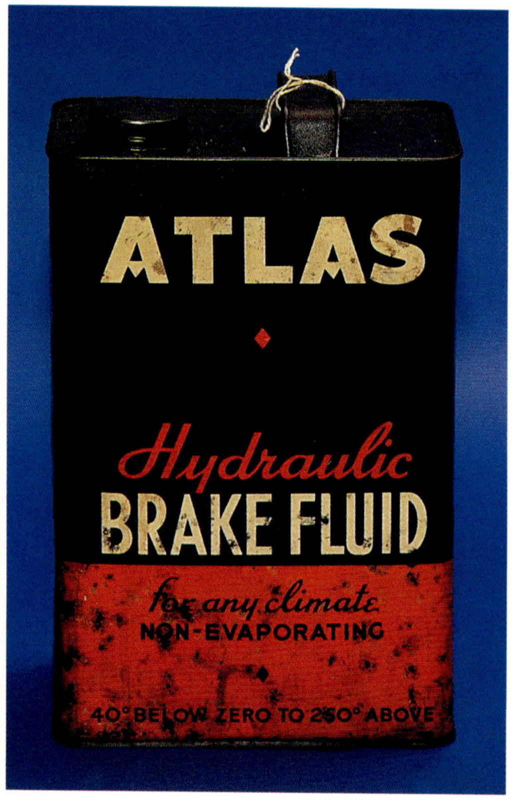

Atlas Brake Fluid, 1-gallon can, 1946. $15-25

Atlas Brake Fluid, 1-gallon cans, 1953 and 1961, $15-25 each.

Left to right: Atlas Brake Fluid, 1-gallon can, 1954, $15-25. Atlas Brake Fluid, 16 oz. cans, 1956, 1961, 1963, $10-20 each.

Atlas Polishing Cloth, 1940s-1963. $10-20 each

Atlas Rubber Lubricant, 1-gallon can, 1963. $15-25

Atlas products, assorted sizes, 1940-1950. $10-20 each

Atlas Tire Tube Repair Kits, 1941-1945. $10-45 each

Atlas Chrome Polish, 8-oz. cans, 1940s-1955. $10-20 each

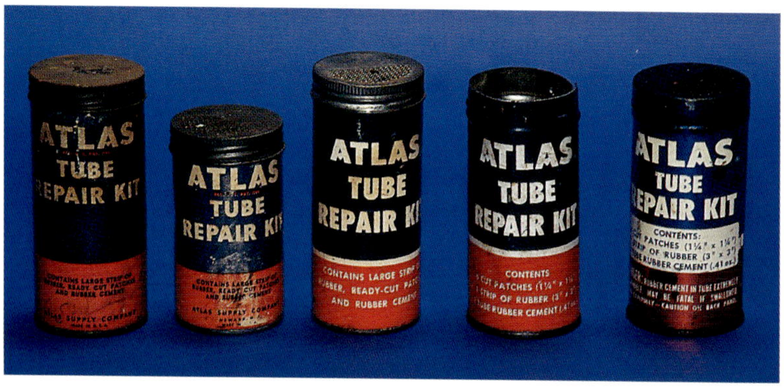

Atlas Tire Tube Repair Kits, 1940-1965. $10-20 each

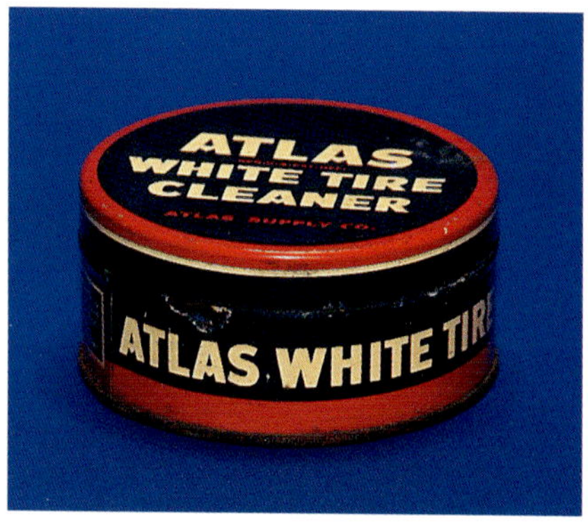

Atlas White Tire Cleaner, 1-lb. can, 1945. $10-20

Atlas Heat Riser Lubricant, 12-oz. cans, 1960-1964. $5-15 each

Atlas products, 1963. $10-15

Atlas car care products, 1969. $10-20 each

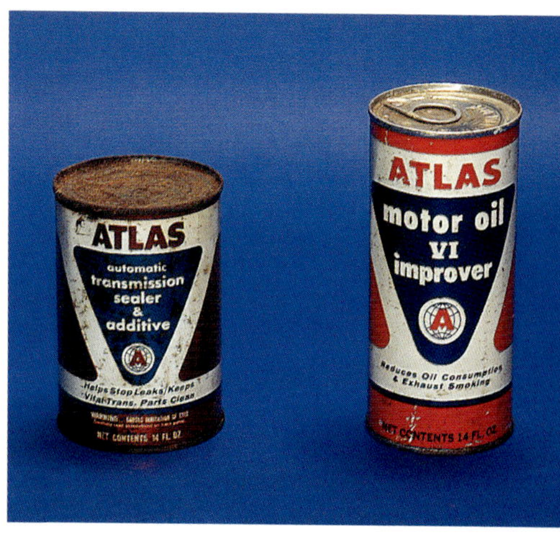

Atlas additives, 1969. $10-20 each

Atlas battery service accessories, 1950s. $125-225 each

Atlas Premium Power display battery, 1969. $25-50

Atlas tire holder, 1931. $75-150

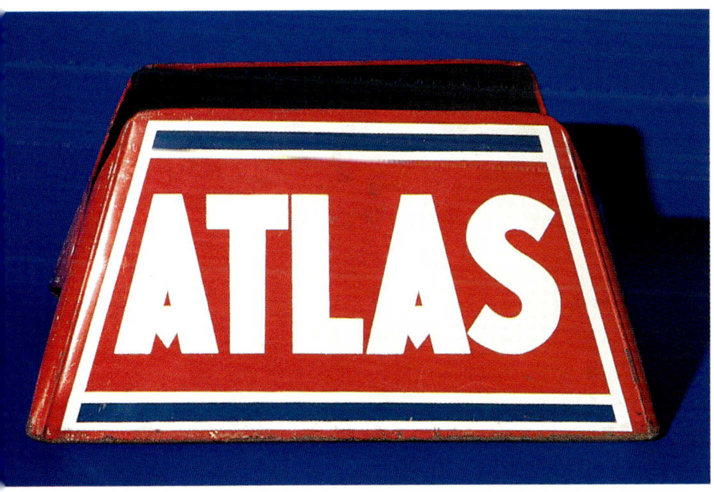

Atlas tire holder, 1941. $75-150

Atlas tire holder with Sohio logo, 1953. $150-250

Sohio/Atlas Tire Holder, 1955. $125-225

Atlas tire holder with Sohio logo, 1959. $150-300

Atlas tire holder with Sohio logo, 1962. $150-250

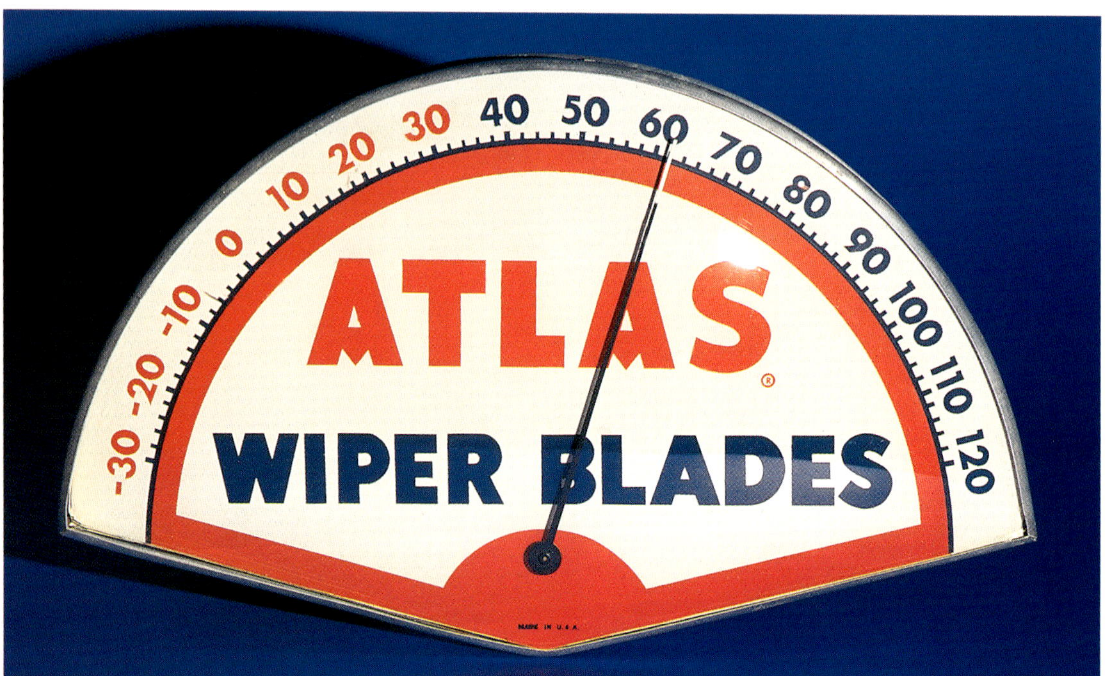

Atlas Wiper Blades thermometer, 1961. $200-275

"Atlas Tires, Guaranteed by Standard Oil Co. of Ohio" building mount sign, 6' x 2', 1931. $500-1,000

"Atlas Tires, Batteries, Accessories" building mount sign, 6' x 3', 1939. $250-300

Atlas tire patch kit and holder, for station use, 1960. $45-65

Atlas 6-volt battery bank, 1949. $35-65

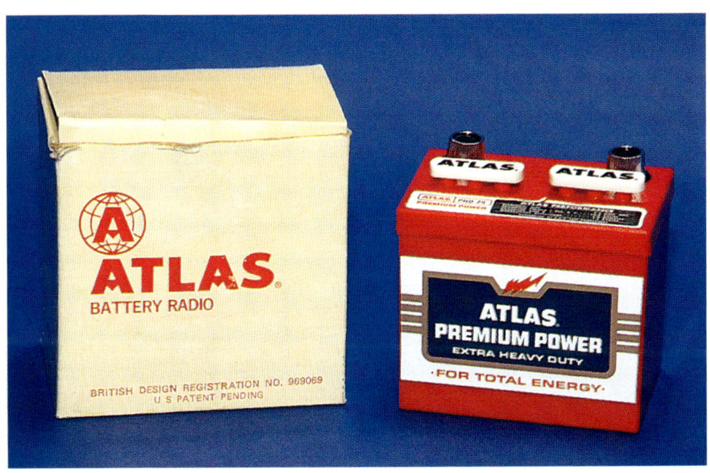

Atlas Premium Power battery radio, 1969. $50-75

Atlas sold a variety of aftermarket parts through Sohio. This is a selection from 1956-1966. $10-20 each

ATLAS
Micronal
GASOLINE FILTER
FF-3
ATLAS
Micronal
GASOLINE FILTER
FF-4
PROTECTS YOUR ENGINE
ATLAS
Micronal
GASOLINE FILTER
FF-7
PROTECTS YOUR ENGINE
ATLAS
GASOLINE FILTER

ATLAS
GREASE SEALS
FOR FRONT WHEELS
ATLAS
Safety
Lift
RADIATOR
PRESSURE CAP
ATLAS
WHEEL
CYLINDER
REPAIR KIT
ATLAS
Locking
GAS CAP

ATLAS
OIL FILTER
KEEPS OIL CLEAN
PROTECTS YOUR ENGINE
ATLAS
Micronic
OIL FILTER REFILL
P-51
ATLAS
Micronal
OIL FILTER
C-21

ATLAS Winter WIPER BLADE
with Self De-Icing blanket · · · FITS BAYONET WIPER ARMS
13" WINTER BLADE
ATLAS Winter WIPER BLADE
with Self De-Icing blanket · · · FITS ALL WIPER ARMS
15" WINTER BLADE
ATLAS Winter WIPER BLADE
FITS ALL WIPER ARMS

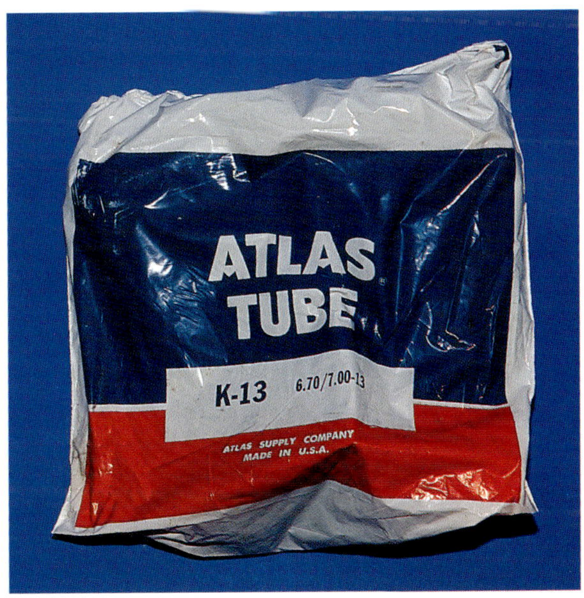
ATLAS
TUBE
K-13 6.70/7.00-13
ATLAS SUPPLY COMPANY
MADE IN U.S.A.

Chapter Seven

Reproduction & Fantasy

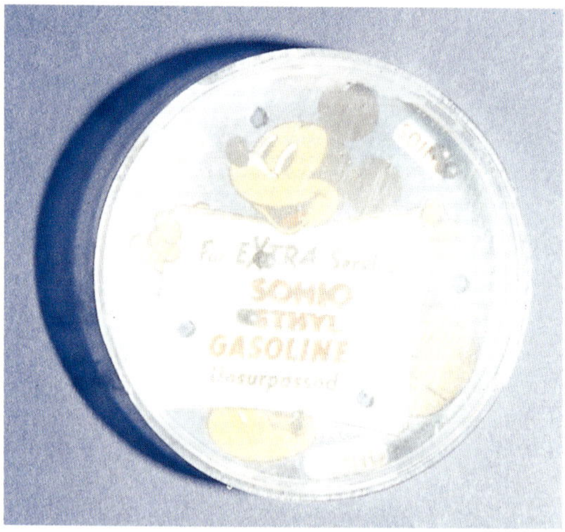

Disney® character Sohio game, fantasy piece. $5-10

Sohio reproduction tin sign, 1933-1945 logo. $10-15

Sohio reproduction steel sign, 1945-1962. $10-15

Sohio paperweight, made from Scott Benjamin's logo book. $5-6

Sohio oil bottle with plastic 1933-1945 logo, $20-25

Sohio Eureka harness oil bottle, possible reproduction. This logo has been reproduced on a variety of bottles. Labels can be soaked in tea for an aged appearance. A large quantity of these bottles has recently flooded the market. No value established

BP has done a lot for the Cleveland community since re-branding, including this amphitheater at the Cleveland Metroparks Zoo.

Appendix

The Other Standard Descendants

The 1911 Supreme Court breakup of Standard Oil created thirty-four separate entities. Standard's net worth of $660 million at the time of the breakup has been surpassed by each of the nine surviving marketing companies detailed in this history, plus several others listed below. These nine were chosen because they are the surviving gasoline marketers, familiar images to the motoring public. But what of the other Standard descendants? Do they survive? Most do, in some form, merged with their former siblings. A few have merged with non-Standard entities until their heritage and identity have been lost. The following chart lists all thirty-four companies and their status at the time of this writing.

1. Standard Oil Company of New Jersey is now Exxon Corporation.
2. Standard Oil Company of New York is now Mobil Corporation.
3. Standard Oil Company of Indiana is now Amoco Corporation.
4. Standard Oil Company of California is now Chevron Corporation.
5. Standard Oil Company of Ohio is now BP America.
6. The Ohio Oil Company is now Marathon Oil, a subsidiary of USX, Inc.
7. The Atlantic Refining Company is now Atlantic Richfield Company.
8. Continental Oil Company is now Conoco, Inc., a subsidiary of Dupont Corporation.
9. South Penn Oil Company is now Pennzoil, Inc.
10. Borne, Scrymser Company survives today as Borne Chemical.
11. Cheesebrough Manufacturing survives today as Cheesebrough-Ponds, Inc., manufacturers of Vaseline products.
12. Washington Oil Company survives as a Pennsylvania oil production firm.
13. Union Tank Car Company survives as a petroleum transportation firm.
14. Buckeye Pipe Line Company survives as a common carrier pipeline today.
15. Vacuum Oil Company merged with Standard of New York in 1931.
16. Standard Oil Company of Nebraska merged with Standard of Indiana in 1939.
17. Standard Oil Company of Kansas merged with Standard of Indiana in 1948.
18. Standard Oil Company of Kentucky merged with Standard of California in 1961.
19. Colonial Oil Company merged with Beacon Oil in 1928, and the combined entity, Colonial Beacon, merged with Standard of New Jersey in 1931.
20. Solar Refining merged with Standard of Ohio in 1931.

21. Anglo-American Oil Company merged with Standard of New Jersey in 1930.
22. Waters Pierce Oil Company became Pierce Petroleum before merging with Sinclair Oil in 1930.
23. Prairie Oil and Gas merged with Sinclair Oil in 1932.
24. Galena-Signal Oil Company merged with Valvoline Oil Company in 1932.
25. Indiana Pipe Line merged with Buckeye Pipe Line in 1942.
26. Northern Pipeline merged with Buckeye Pipe Line in 1964.
27. New York Transit merged with Buckeye Pipe Line in 1964.
28. South-West Pennsylvania Pipelines merged with National Transit in 1952.
29. National Transit merged with South Penn Oil Company in 1965.
30. Eureka Pipe Line merged with South Penn Oil Company in 1947.
31. Cumberland Pipe Line merged with Ashland Oil in 1931.
32. Southern Pipe Line merged with Ashland Oil in 1949.
33. Crescent Pipe Line did not survive the Great Depression.
34. Swan and Finch survived as an industrial lubricants manufacturer until the 1960s.

As you can see, Standard descendants tended to form alliances with their former siblings. Only Sinclair, with close ties to Standard of Indiana, and Ashland/Valvoline, with close ties to Standard of Ohio, have had any significant relationships with the Standard descendants. Of the thirty-four companies, only two appear to have completely liquidated. It is likely that Standard descendants acquired assets of these companies as well, but that cannot be determined at this time.

The threat of monopolization of America's petroleum industry, so deftly eliminated by the government in 1911, was hardly a threat at all. Many of the Standard siblings have long since surpassed the parent company in assets and net worth. Indeed, the petroleum industry, even the entire twentieth century, would have been different had there been no Standard. Standard was the fuel—and the lubricant—for the industrialization in the nineteenth century and the mobilization in the twentieth century of the world.

Important Dates In Sohio History

April 1928	Sohio name adopted.
April 1928	Fleet-Wing organized
June 1928	First modern service center
Aug. 1928	Purchase Latonia Refinery
April 1929	Purchase Cadwell & Taylor
June 1930	Tires added to product line (Atlas)
April 1931	Sohio X70 introduced
1931	Purchased Solar Refining
Oct. 17, 1931	Sohio Hi-So green gasoline introduced
Nov. 1931	Purchased Refiners Oil Co.
Oct. 1935	Sohio starts selling Esso motor oil
1936	Guaranteed starting introduced
July 1939	Sohio Supreme introduced
Oct. 1939	Atlas Perma-Guard anti-freeze introduced

Jan. 1940	70th anniversary
July 1941	Sohio So-Clear introduced
Sept. 1945	Purchase Canfield Oil Co.
Nov. 1946	Sohio Tone introduced
March 1947	Sohio HQ motor oil introduced
March 1950	Sohio Xtane introduced
Sept. 1950	Barge Fleet eliminated
Aug. 1951	Sohio HQD introduced
May 1953	Sohio sells Esso Uniflo motor oil
Oct. 1954	New Sohio Boron Supreme gasoline
Jan. 10, 1955	Sohio issues one share of stock to every baby born on this date for 85 years in business.
Feb. 28, 1955	Atlas tubeless tires introduced
June 1955	Sohio Boron introduced
July 25, 1955	Sohio Premex introduced at $.60 per quart
Nov. 1955	Canfield stations re-branded to Sohio
Oct. 1956	New Boron Super Premium gasoline
March 1956	Premex 5-quart can introduced
1956-1958	Construction of Toledo Refinery
May 15, 1957	Sohio introduces $100,000 baseball jackpot
May 1957	Sohio Lubtec introduced
May 5, 1958	Sohio Extron gasoline introduced
May 21, 1958	Sohio $200,000 family jackpot
Nov. 1, 1958	Sohio S-3HD motor oil introduced
Oct. 1960	Sohio Tran Grease cartridge introduced
Nov. 10, 1961	New logo first appears in print. Although the new logo first appeared in print in 1961, it was not widely used until 1962, so items of this vintage are thought of as 1962 vintage and on.
March 1962	Sohio Duron introduced
Apr. 7, 1962	Sohio Diesel Supreme introduced
May 12, 1963	Sohio $250,000 license plate jackpot
Nov. 15, 1963	Sohio Frostex discontinued and replaced with Atlas Gas Line Antifreeze
Jan. 2, 1964	Sohio Lubtec 5 and 10 lb. cans discontinued
May 24, 1964	Sohio $300,000 license plate jackpot
March 1966	Sohio $200,000 license plate jackpot
May 17, 1965	Sohio $350,000 license plate jackpot
June 1, 1966	Automatic transmission fluid gallon cans discontinued
June 6, 1966	Sohio $300,000 license plate jackpot
Nov. 28, 1966	Sohio Top Dollar license plate jackpot
July 1, 1967	Polarine two-gallon can discontinued
July 1, 1967	Sohio HQD discontinued
July 1, 1967	Sohio motor oil discontinued
July 1, 1967	Sohio 4-cycle motor oil discontinued
July 1, 1967	Sohio Sixty Two motor oil replaces HQD
1967	Sohio Cash-in-a-Flash game (black tickets)
Nov. 1967	Sohio Super Cash-in-a-Flash game
Apr. 2, 1968	Sohio Pay-Day card game
Oct. 1969	Sohio Cash-in-a-Flash game (green tickets)
Aug. 1969	Boron Bonanza card game
Feb. 1, 1989	Sohio stations branded BP

Names and Trademarks

Sohio items from 1964-on are sometimes hard to spot. Here is a list of some Sohio brand names and trademarks, from 1928 - 1989.

Valve Ease
Frostex
So-Clear
Guaranteed Starting
Guaranteed Radiator Protection
Lubri Check
Point by Point Lubrication
Lubtec
Lubtec L
SohioSpin
HI-CYL
Sohiolube
Ice Guard
Farmcx
7C' s
Super 7C's Multi Duty
Super Sohio
Herd Oil
Sohio Heat

Parowax
Eureka Harness Oil
Sohiotone
Sohioseal
Sohio Motor Oil
Standard Oil Penn
Sohio HQ
Sohio HQD
Sohio Premex
Sohio Duron
Sohio Golden Duron
Sohio QVO
Sohio Sixty-Two
Sohio Nitrex
Sohio Octron HD
Sohio Cetron HD
Sohio CHD
Sohio Facto
Sohio Dieselube M
Sohio HD

Sohio HD - S3
Sohio Dieselube 310
Sohio Dieselube 330
Sohio HD-S1
Renown
Polarine
Multron
Nitron
Acme
Sohio Secretary Service

Industrial

Sohio 78 Grease
Sohio Stoddard Solvent
Sohio Staysol
Sohiokut S-4
Varnolene 3039
Gear EP

Factran Grease (MP)
Bearing Gard Multi Service Grease
Eldoran (SP) Lubricant
Factovolt
Industron
Factran
Factoway
Factokut
Factorg 101
Factokote
Factopor
Factoquench 74
Startic
Sulkleer
Tolvol
Staysol
Aromatic Solvent 100/150
SohioGro

Resources

Trade Publications for Collectors

Petroleum Collectibles Monthly
411 Forest Street
LaGrange, OH 44050
(440) 355-6608, Fax (440) 355-4955

Check the Oil
PO Box 937
Powell, OH 43065-0937
(614) 848-5038

Buyer and Appraisals of Sohio Items

W. Clark Miller
9944 Gardenside Drive
Waite Hill, OH 44094-6979
(440) 942-3386, (440) 942-1079

Gas Pumps, Parts, and Restorations

Vic's Place
124 North 2nd
Gutherie, OK 73044
(405) 282-5586

Bibliography

Scott Benjamin and Wayne Henderson. *Gas Globes: Pennzoil to Union 76 Affiliates*. Atglen, Pennsylvania. Schiffer Publishing, Ltd., 1999.

Scott Benjamin and Wayne Henderson. *Standard Oil, the First 125 Years*. Osceola, WI. Motor Books International, 1996.

McIntyre, J. Sam. *The Esso Collectibles Handbook*: *Memorabilia of Standard Oil of New Jersey*. Atglen, Pennsylvania. Schiffer Publishing, Ltd., 1998.

Russell, Mark. "BP Logo to Cover all Stations". *The Cleveland Plain Dealer*, Cleveland, Ohio. Feb. 1, 1989.

Standard Oil Company (Ohio). 75th Anniversary magazine, January 10, 1945. Cleveland, Ohio. Standard Oil Company of Ohio, 1945.

Standard Oil Company (Ohio) *Sohioan*, January 1940, 70th Anniversary Number 1870-1940. Cleveland, Ohio. Standard Oil Company. 1940.

Standard Oil Company (Ohio). *The Sohioan* Centennial Issue, 1870-1970. January 1970. Cleveland, Ohio. Standard Oil Company. 1970.